**Managing Editor**
Mara Ellen Guckian

**Editor in Chief**
Karen J. Goldfluss, M.S. Ed.

**Creative Director**
Sarah M. Fournier

**Cover Artist**
Sarah Kim

**Imaging**
Leonard P. Swierski

**Publisher**
Mary D. Smith, M.S. Ed.

Teacher Created Resources
TCR 8079

MW00338717

MI...
MA...

# TIMED MATH PRACTICE

*Test 10*

Numbers

- Contains **100** timed tests for practice in key areas.
- Presents multiple methods for solving standards-based problems.
- Enhances math speed and fluency.

Teacher Created Resources

For correlations to the Common Core State Standards, see page 105 of this book or visit *http://www.teachercreated.com/standards/*.

## Teacher Created Resources

12621 Western Avenue
Garden Grove, CA 92841
www.teachercreated.com
ISBN: 978-1-4206-8079-9
© 2017 Teacher Created Resources
Made in U.S.A.

Teacher Created Resources

# Table of Contents

# Introduction

The *Minutes to Mastery* series was designed to help students build confidence in their math abilities during testing situations. As students develop fluency with math facts and operations, they improve their abilities to do different types of math problems comfortably and quickly.

Each of the 100 tests in this book has 10 questions in key math areas. Multiple opportunities are presented to solve the standards-based problems while developing speed and fluency. The pages present problems in a variety of ways using different terminology. For instance, in subtraction, students might be asked to *subtract* or to *find the difference*. Terms like *less* and *minus* are both used to ensure that students are comfortable with different phrasings. Word problems are included to provide additional practice decoding text for clues. Critical thinking and abstract reasoning play such an important role in solving math problems, and practice is imperative.

Keep in mind, timing can sometimes add to the stress of learning. If this is the case for your math learner(s), don't focus on timing in the beginning. As confidence in the process of answering a number of different types of questions builds, so will accuracy and speed. Then you can introduce timing.

Establish a timing system that works well for your group. Here are steps to help you get started:

1. Present a worksheet without officially timing it to get a sense of how long it will take to complete—perhaps 10 minutes. Ideally, you want all ten questions per page to be answered.

2. Allow students to practice using the preferred timer before taking a timed test.

3. Remind students to write their answers neatly.

4. Take a few timed tests and see how it works. Adjust the time as needed.

5. Work to improve the number of correct answers within the given time. Remind students that it is important to be accurate, not just fast!

6. Encourage students to try to do their best each time, to review their results, and to spend time working on areas where they had difficulties. The Tracking Sheet can be used to record the number of correct answers for each test. The final column can be used for the date the test was taken or for initials.

The section at the bottom of each page can be used to record specific progress on that test, including the time the student started the test, finished the test, the total time taken, how many problems were completed, and how many problems were correct.

Hopefully, with practice, all students will begin challenging themselves to go faster, while remaining accurate and writing clearly.

# Tracking Sheet

Name _____

| Numbers (Review 1–10) | | |
|---|---|---|
| Test 1 | /10 | |
| Test 2 | /10 | |
| Test 3 | /10 | |
| Test 4 | /10 | |
| Test 5 | /10 | |
| Test 6 | /10 | |
| Test 7 | /10 | |
| Test 8 | /10 | |
| Test 9 | /10 | |
| Test 10 | /10 | |
| Test 11 | /10 | |
| Operations in Base 10 | | |
| Test 12 | /10 | |
| Test 13 | /10 | |
| Test 14 | /10 | |
| Test 15 | /10 | |
| Test 16 | /10 | |
| Test 17 | /10 | |
| Test 18 | /10 | |
| Test 19 | /10 | |
| Test 20 | /10 | |
| Test 21 | /10 | |
| Test 22 | /10 | |
| Greater Than, Less Than, Equal To | | |
| Test 23 | /10 | |
| Test 24 | /10 | |
| Test 25 | /10 | |
| Test 26 | /10 | |
| Test 27 | /10 | |
| Number Lines | | |
| Test 28 | /10 | |
| Test 29 | /10 | |
| Test 30 | /10 | |
| Addition | | |
| Test 31 | /10 | |
| Test 32 | /10 | |
| Test 33 | /10 | |

| Test 34 | /10 | |
|---|---|---|
| Test 35 | /10 | |
| Test 36 | /10 | |
| Test 37 | /10 | |
| Test 38 | /10 | |
| Test 39 | /10 | |
| Test 40 | /10 | |
| Test 41 | /10 | |
| Test 42 | /10 | |
| Subtraction | | |
| Test 43 | /10 | |
| Test 44 | /10 | |
| Test 45 | /10 | |
| Test 46 | /10 | |
| Test 47 | /10 | |
| Test 48 | /10 | |
| Test 49 | /10 | |
| Test 50 | /10 | |
| Test 51 | /10 | |
| Test 52 | /10 | |
| Test 53 | /10 | |
| Test 54 | /10 | |
| Mixed Equations | | |
| Test 55 | /10 | |
| Test 56 | /10 | |
| Test 57 | /10 | |
| Test 58 | /10 | |
| Test 59 | /10 | |
| Test 60 | /10 | |
| Measurement | | |
| Test 61 | /10 | |
| Test 62 | /10 | |
| Test 63 | /10 | |
| Test 64 | /10 | |
| Test 65 | /10 | |
| Test 66 | /10 | |
| Test 67 | /10 | |
| Test 68 | /10 | |

| Test 69 | /10 | |
|---|---|---|
| Time | | |
| Test 70 | /10 | |
| Test 71 | /10 | |
| Test 72 | /10 | |
| Test 73 | /10 | |
| Test 74 | /10 | |
| Test 75 | /10 | |
| Interpret Data | | |
| Test 76 | /10 | |
| Test 77 | /10 | |
| Test 78 | /10 | |
| Test 79 | /10 | |
| Test 80 | /10 | |
| Geometry | | |
| Test 81 | /10 | |
| Test 82 | /10 | |
| Test 83 | /10 | |
| Test 84 | /10 | |
| Test 85 | /10 | |
| Test 86 | /10 | |
| Symmetry | | |
| Test 87 | /10 | |
| Test 88 | /10 | |
| Test 89 | /10 | |
| Fractions | | |
| Test 90 | /10 | |
| Test 91 | /10 | |
| Test 92 | /10 | |
| Test 93 | /10 | |
| Test 94 | /10 | |
| Test 95 | /10 | |
| Money | | |
| Test 96 | /10 | |
| Test 97 | /10 | |
| Test 98 | /10 | |
| Test 99 | /10 | |
| Test 100 | /10 | |

Name _____     Date _____

## Write the number word for each number.

**1.** 2 _____

**2.** 5 _____

**3.** 1 _____

**4.** 4 _____

**5.** 3 _____

## Count the dots on each domino and write the number and number word for each one.

**6.**    **Number** _____    **Number Word** _____

**7.**    **Number** _____    **Number Word** _____

**8.**    **Number** _____    **Number Word** _____

**9.**    **Number** _____    **Number Word** _____

**10.**    **Number** _____    **Number Word** _____

| Started: | Finished: | Total Time: | Completed: | Correct: |
|----------|-----------|-------------|------------|----------|

Name _____ Date _____

## Circle groups of 2. How many groups did you find in each row?

1.    _____ groups

2.  _____ groups

3.      _____ groups

## Solve the addition problems.

4. 2 + 2 = _____

5. 2 + 3 = _____

6. 2 + 1 = _____

7. 2 + 4 = _____

8. 2 + 6 = _____

## Count by 2s.

9. How many slippers are there altogether? _____

10. How many slippers are there altogether? _____

| Started: | Finished: | Total Time: | Completed: | Correct: |  |
|---|---|---|---|---|---|

Name _____  Date _____

## Circle groups of 3.  How many groups did you find in each row?

**1.** ☆☆☆☆☆☆☆☆☆ _____ **groups**

**2.** ☆☆☆ _____ **group**

**3.** ☆☆☆☆☆☆☆☆☆☆☆☆ _____ **groups**

**4.** ☆☆☆☆☆☆ _____ **groups**

## The number 3 is an odd number.  Circle the other odd numbers in each row.

**5.**  5    4    1    6    9    11

**6.**  1    2    7    13    5    8

## Cross out the correct insect in each row.

**7.** 2nd insect

**8.** 4th insect

**9.** 1st insect

**10.** 3rd insect

| Started: | Finished: | Total Time: | Completed: | Correct: |
|---|---|---|---|---|

Name _____    Date _____

## Circle groups of 4.  How many groups did you find in each row?

1. ☆ ☆ ☆ ☆ ☆ ☆ ☆ ☆ _____ **groups**

2. ☆ ☆ ☆ ☆ _____ **group**

3. ☆ ☆ ☆ ☆ ☆ ☆ ☆ ☆ ☆ ☆ ☆ ☆ _____ **groups**

## Solve the addition problems.

**4.** $2 + 4 =$ _____    **5.** $4 + 4 =$ _____

**6.** $1 + 4 =$ _____    **7.** $4 + 5 =$ _____

## How many butterflies are in each group?

**8.** _____ **butterflies**

**9.** _____ **butterflies**

**10.** _____ **butterflies**

| Started: | Finished: | Total Time: | Completed: | Correct: |
|---|---|---|---|---|

Name _____　　Date _____

**Use the word bank to write the word for each ordinal number.**

| first | second | third |
|-------|--------|-------|
| fourth | | fifth |

**1.** 2nd _____

**2.** 4th _____

**3.** 1st _____

**4.** 5th _____

**5.** 3rd _____

**Solve the addition problems.**

**6.**　　3　　　　　　　**7.**　　4　　　　　　**8.**　　2
　　　+ 2　　　　　　　　　+ 3　　　　　　　　　+ 4

**Fill in the missing odd numbers.**

**9.** _____, 2, _____, 4, _____, 6, _____, 8, _____, 10

**Fill in the missing even numbers.**

**10.** 1, _____, 3, _____, 5, _____, 7, _____, 9, _____

| Started: | Finished: | Total Time: | Completed: | Correct: |
|----------|-----------|-------------|------------|----------|

Name _____          Date _____

## Circle groups of 5.  How many groups did you find in each row?

| 1. | • • • • • • • •  • • • • • • • •  _____ groups |
| 2. | • • • • •  • • • • •  • • • • •  _____ groups |
| 3. | • • • • •  • • • • •  • • • • •  _____ groups |

## Solve the addition problems.

**4.** 2 + 3 = _____          **5.** 1 + 4 = _____

**6.**    5                          **7.**    5
      + 0                                + 5
     _____                               _____

## How many nuts does each squirrel have?

| 8. 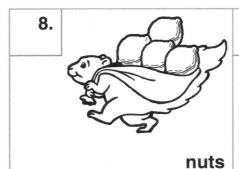 _____ nuts | 9.  _____ nuts | 10.  _____ nuts |

| Started: | Finished: | Total Time: | Completed: | Correct: |  |

Name _____    Date _____

**Circle groups of 6.  How many groups did you find in each row?**

1. _____ groups

2. _____ group

3. _____ groups

**Circle groups of 7.  How many groups did you find in each row?**

4. _____ groups

5. _____ groups

6. _____ group

**Solve the addition problems.  Circle the one that equals 9.**

| 7. | 5 | 8. | 3 | 9. | 7 | 10. | 6 |
|----|----|----|----|----|----|----|----|
|    | + 2 |    | + 3 |    | + 2 |    | + 4 |

| Started: | Finished: | Total Time: | Completed: | Correct: |
|----------|-----------|-------------|------------|----------|

Name _____    Date _____

**Circle groups of 8.  How many groups of 8 did you find?**

1. ✔✔✔✔✔✔✔✔✔✔✔✔✔✔

   ✔✔✔✔✔✔✔✔✔✔✔✔✔✔ _____ **groups**

**Solve the addition problems.**

2. $4 + 4 =$ _____     3. $5 + 3 =$ _____     4. $8 + 2 =$ _____

**Circle groups of 9.  How many groups of 9 did you find?**

5. ✔ ✔ ✔ ✔ ✔ ✔ ✔ ✔ ✔

   ✔ ✔ ✔ ✔ ✔ ✔ ✔ ✔ ✔

   ✔ ✔ ✔ ✔ ✔ ✔ ✔ ✔ ✔ _____ **groups**

**Solve the addition problems.**

6.    6
     + 3

7.    5
     + 4

8.    2
     + 7

**Answer the questions.**

9. What is $8 + 8$? _____     10. What is $9 + 9$? _____

| Started: | Finished: | Total Time: | Completed: | Correct: |
|---|---|---|---|---|

Name _____  Date _____

**Count the 10 chicks.  Circle groups of 2.  How many groups of 2 did you circle?**

1.

_____ groups

**Circle groups of 5.  How many groups of 5 did you circle?**

2.

_____ groups

**Draw a group of 10 triangles.**

3.
```
┌─────────────────────────────────────────┐
│                                         │
│                                         │
│                                         │
└─────────────────────────────────────────┘
```

**Fill in the blanks in each row to count by 10.**

4. 10, _____, 30, 40, _____, 60, _____, 80, _____, 100

5. 10, 20, _____, 40, 50, _____, _____, 80, _____, 100

**Add the happy faces.**

6.      +    = _____

7.   +      = _____

**Read the questions.  Write and solve the problems.**

8. What is seven plus three? _____

9. What is five plus five? _____

10. What is four plus six? _____

| Started: | Finished: | Total Time: | Completed: | Correct: |
|---|---|---|---|---|

Name _____    Date _____

## Count the socks by 2s.

**1.** How many socks are there altogether?

_____ **socks**

**2.** Cross out two pairs of socks. How many socks are left?

_____ **socks**

## How many tens and ones are in each group?

**3.**

| Tens | Ones |
|------|------|
|      |      |

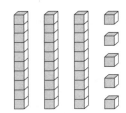

**4.**

| Tens | Ones |
|------|------|
|      |      |

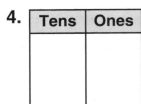 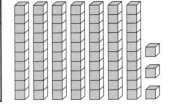

## Follow the directions for each question.

**5.** Circle the *fifth* shirt.

**6.** Cross out the *third* shirt.

**7.** Draw circles around the *odd* numbers.

   2    3    4    5    6    7    8    9    10

**8.** Cross out the *even* numbers.

   2    3    4    5    6    7    8    9    10

**9.** Which is the *largest* number?

   2    8    20    9    15    0    7    11    4

**10.** Which is the *smallest* number?

   3    6    20    12    17    8    10    16    2

| Started: | Finished: | Total Time: | Completed: | Correct: |
|----------|-----------|-------------|------------|----------|

Name _____ Date _____

## Solve the doubles.

| **1.** | 5 | | **2.** | 4 | | **3.** | 3 |
|---|---|---|---|---|---|---|---|
| | + 5 | | | + 4 | | | + 3 |

## Write the number for each number word.

**4.** seven _____

**5.** ten _____

**6.** four _____

**7.** nine _____

## Fill in the missing numbers to complete the problems below.

**8.** $6 +$ _____ $= 9$

**9.** _____ $+ 4 = 10$

**10.** $5 +$ _____ $= 7$

| Started: | Finished: | Total Time: | Completed: | Correct: |
|---|---|---|---|---|

Name _____ Date _____

**How many ones ( ◻ ) are in each row? Count them.**

1. ◻◻◻◻◻ There are _____ ones.

2. ◻◻◻◻ There are _____ ones.

3. ◻◻◻◻◻◻◻ There are _____ ones.

4. ◻◻◻◻◻ There are _____ ones.

5. ◻◻ There are _____ ones.

**Count the ones ( ◻ ) and circle the correct number in each row.**

6. ◻◻◻     1 2 3 4 5 6 7 8 9

7. ◻◻◻◻◻◻     1 2 3 4 5 6 7 8 9

8. ◻◻◻◻     1 2 3 4 5 6 7 8 9

9. ◻◻◻◻◻◻◻◻◻ 1 2 3 4 5 6 7 8 9

**Add the ones.**

10. ◻◻◻ + ◻◻ + ◻◻◻◻ = _____

| Started: | Finished: | Total Time: | Completed: | Correct: |
|----------|-----------|-------------|------------|----------|

Name _____　Date _____

## How many tens (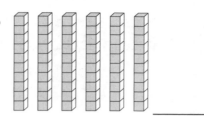) are in each group?  Count them.

**1.** 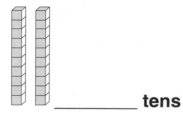 _____ tens

**2.** _____ tens

**3.** _____ tens

**4.** _____ tens

## Circle the correct number of groups of 10.  Write the total on the line.

**5.** 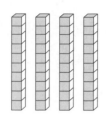　　1　2　3　4　5　6　7　8　9　= _____

**6.** 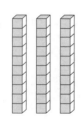　　1　2　3　4　5　6　7　8　9　= _____

## Add to solve the problems.

**7.** 10 + 10 = _____　　　　**8.** 10 + 10 + 10 + 10 = _____

**9.** 10 + 10 + 10 = _____　　**10.** 10 + 10 + 10 + 10 + 10 = _____

| Started: | Finished: | Total Time: | Completed: | Correct: |
|----------|-----------|-------------|------------|----------|

Name _____    Date _____

This 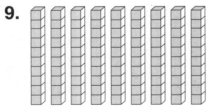 equals 10.  How many tens are in each group?

1. 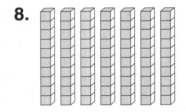 _____ tens

2. _____ tens

3. _____ tens

**Add to solve the problems.  (Hint:  Count by 10s!)**

4. 10 + 10 + 10 + 10 + 10 + 10 = _____

5. 10 + 10 + 10 + 10 + 10 + 10 + 10 = _____

6. 10 + 10 + 10 + 10 + 10 + 10 + 10 + 10 + 10 = _____

7. 10 + 10 + 10 + 10 = _____

**Count the tens and circle the correct number in each row.**

8. 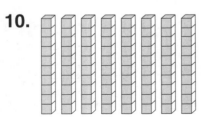    10   20   30   40   50   60   70   80   90

9.    10   20   30   40   50   60   70   80   90

10.    10   20   30   40   50   60   70   80   90

| Started: | Finished: | Total Time: | Completed: | Correct: |
|---|---|---|---|---|

# Test 15     Operations in Base Ten

Name _____ Date _____

**Write the following numbers in expanded notation. The first one has been started for you.**

**1.** 13 = _____**10**_____ + _____     **2.** 68 = _____ + _____

**3.** 45 = _____ + _____     **4.** 79 = _____ + _____

**5.** 21 = _____ + _____     **6.** 36 = _____ + _____

**Count the tens (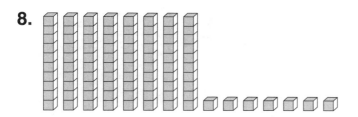) and ones (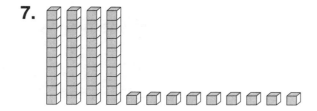).**

**7.**

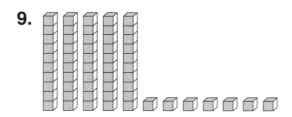

_____ Tens _____ Ones

**8.**

_____ Tens _____ Ones

**9.**

_____ Tens _____ Ones

**10.**

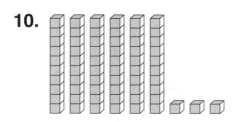

_____ Tens _____ Ones

| Started: | Finished: | Total Time: | Completed: | Correct: |
|----------|-----------|-------------|------------|----------|

Name _____ Date _____

## How many tens and ones do you need for each number?

**1.** 35 _____ **Tens** + _____ **Ones**

**2.** 89 _____ **Tens** + _____ **Ones**

**3.** 42 _____ **Tens** + _____ **Ones**

**4.** 11 _____ **Ten** + _____ **One**

**5.** 57 _____ **Tens** + _____ **Ones**

**Count the groups of tens (▱▱▱▱▱) and ones (◻).  Fill in the boxes and then write the whole number on the line.**

**6.**

 = 

| Tens | Ones |
|------|------|

= _____

**7.**

= 

| Ten | Ones |
|-----|------|

= _____

**Change the number words to numbers.  Then write each number in expanded notation.**

**8.** eleven _____ = _____ + _____

**9.** twelve _____ = _____ + _____

**10.** fourteen _____ = _____ + _____

| Started: | Finished: | Total Time: | Completed: | Correct: |
|----------|-----------|-------------|------------|----------|

Name _____    Date _____

**Fill in the missing numbers to count by 10.**

1. 10, _____, 30, _____, 50, _____, 70, _____, 90, 100

2. _____, 20, _____, _____, 50, 60, 70, _____, 90, 100

3. 10, 20, _____, 40, _____, 60, _____, 80, _____, 100

4. 10, _____, 30, 40, 50, _____, _____, 80, 90, _____

**Write the following numbers in expanded notation.**

5. 26 = _____ + _____

6. 37 = _____ + _____

7. 48 = _____ + _____

**Circle the numbers that you say when you count by 10s.**

8.     12       30       45       50       20       96

**Circle the numbers that have a one in the tens place.**

9.     15       21       12       31       14       41

**Circle the numbers that have a four in the ones place.**

10.    11       51       74       43       34       41

| Started: | Finished: | Total Time: | Completed: | Correct: |
| --- | --- | --- | --- | --- |

Name _____    Date _____

**Circle the numbers that have a five in the ones place.**

1.    15      50      45      57      25      87

**Circle the numbers that have a three in the ones place.**

2.    13      31      73      54      34      83

**Circle the number with the most tens.**

3.    88      89      99      77      79      59

**Circle the number that has 8 tens and no ones.**

4.    28      82      18      86      80      58

**Circle the number that has 5 tens and 3 ones.**

5.    50      52      35      53      30      15

**Circle the number that has 2 tens and 7 ones.**

6.    17      72      12      53      27      37

**Change the number words to numbers. Then write each number in expanded notation.**

7. fifteen _____ = _____ + _____

8. fifty-one _____ = _____ + _____

9. sixty-four _____ = _____ + _____

10. seventy-eight _____ = _____ + _____

| Started: | Finished: | Total Time: | Completed: | Correct: |
|---|---|---|---|---|

# Operations in Base Ten

Name _____ Date _____

**Fill in the missing numbers in each row.  Then circle all the 10s.**

1.   1   [ ]   3   4   [ ]   6   7   8   9   [ ]

2.   11   12   [ ]   14   15   [ ]   17   18   [ ]   20

3.   21   [ ]   23   [ ]   25   26   27   [ ]   29   30

4.   31   32   [ ]   34   [ ]   36   [ ]   38   39   40

5.   [ ]   42   [ ]   44   45   [ ]   47   48   49   50

6.   51   52   53   54   [ ]   56   [ ]   58   59   [ ]

7.   61   62   63   [ ]   65   66   67   [ ]   [ ]   70

8.   71   72   [ ]   74   [ ]   76   77   78   [ ]   80

9.   81   [ ]   83   84   85   [ ]   87   88   89   90

10.   [ ]   92   93   [ ]   95   96   97   98   99

| Started: | Finished: | Total Time: | Completed: | Correct: |
|---|---|---|---|---|

Name _____    Date _____

**What does each block or group of base 10 blocks equal?**

**1.** ▭ = _____

**2.** = _____

**3.** = _____

**4.** = _____

**Write the number of hundreds, tens, and ones.**

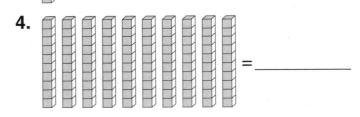

Another way to show 100 is with a [block] block.

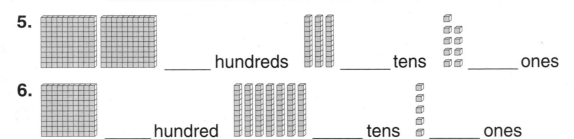

**5.** _____ hundreds _____ tens _____ ones

**6.** _____ hundred _____ tens _____ ones

**7.** _____ hundreds _____ tens _____ ones

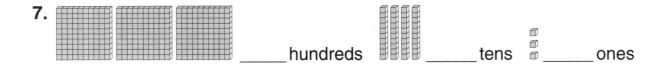

**How many hundreds are in each number below?**

**8.** 908 has _____ hundreds

**9.** 786 has _____ hundreds

**10.** 567 has _____ hundreds

| Started: | Finished: | Total Time: | Completed: | Correct: |
| --- | --- | --- | --- | --- |

Name _____ Date _____

**Circle the number that has a six in the hundreds place.**

1.    846      562      601

**Circle the number that has a two in the hundreds place.**

2.    123      231      312

**Circle the number that has a five in the hundreds place.**

3.    508      850      855

**Circle the number that has a nine in the hundreds place.**

4.    696      969      609

**Use the base 10 blocks to figure out each number.**

5. _____

6. _____

7. _____

**Match the numbers in the box to the number words below.**

| 156 | 349 | 202 |
|-----|-----|-----|

8. three hundred forty-nine _____

9. one hundred fifty-six _____

10. two hundred two _____

| Started: | Finished: | Total Time: | Completed: | Correct: |
|----------|-----------|-------------|------------|----------|

Name _____    Date _____

**Use the base 10 blocks to figure out each number.**

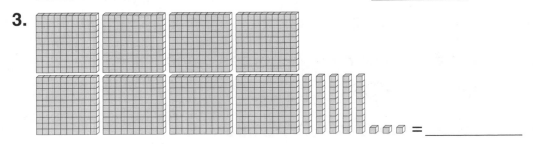

1. _____ = _____

2. _____ = _____

3. _____ = _____

4. _____ = _____

**Circle the number that has a one in the hundreds place.**

5.    141        514        441

**Circle the number that has a two in the ones place.**

6.    123        132        213

**Circle the number that has a five in the hundreds place and a five in the tens place.**

7.    500        505        550

**Answer each question.**

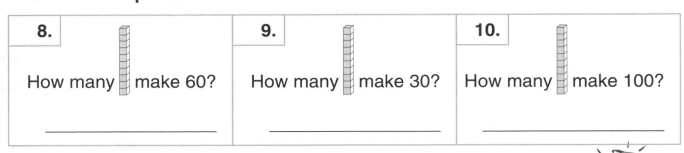

| 8. How many ▯ make 60? | 9. How many ▯ make 30? | 10. How many ▯ make 100? |
|---|---|---|
| _____ | _____ | _____ |

| Started: | Finished: | Total Time: | Completed: | Correct: |

# Greater Than

Name _____ Date _____

**Circle the mitten that has the *larger* number in each pair.**

| 1. |  | 2. |  |
|----|------|----|------|
| 3. | 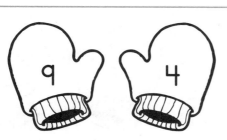 | 4. | 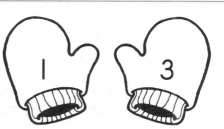 |

**Circle the *largest* number in each row.**

| 5. | 11 | 15 | 12 | 20 | 9 |
|----|----|----|----|----|----|
| 6. | 30 | 33 | 35 | 39 | 37 |
| 7. | 44 | 22 | 66 | 33 | 77 |
| 8. | 98 | 89 | 99 | 96 | 69 |

**Write these numbers in order from *largest to smallest*.**

| 12 | 15 | 9 | 19 | 14 |
|----|----|----|----|----|

9. _____  _____  _____  _____  _____

**10.** Which number was the *largest* in problem 9? _____

| Started: | Finished: | Total Time: | Completed: | Correct: |
|----------|-----------|-------------|------------|----------|

Name _____     Date _____

**Circle the mitten that has the *smaller* number in each pair.**

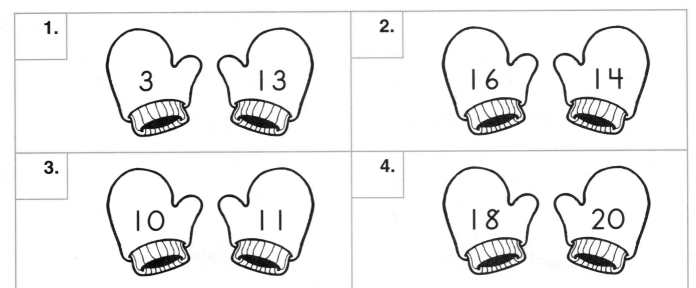

1. 3    13
2. 16    14
3. 10    11
4. 18    20

**Circle the *smallest* number in each row.**

| 5. | 11 | 15 | 12 | 20 | 9 |
| 6. | 30 | 33 | 35 | 39 | 37 |
| 7. | 44 | 22 | 66 | 33 | 77 |
| 8. | 62 | 16 | 13 | 26 | 12 |

**Write these numbers in order from *smallest to largest*.**

| 11 | 8 | 20 | 16 | 18 |

9. _____  _____  _____  _____  _____

10. Which number was the *smallest* in problem 9? _____

| Started: | Finished: | Total Time: | Completed: | Correct: |

# Test 25   Greater Than, Less Than

Name _____   Date _____

> The sign for *greater than* is > .  The sign for *less than* is < .

**Count the shapes in each group.  Put the correct sign ( > or < ) between each group.**

1.

2.

3.

**Compare the numbers on each line.  Put the correct sign ( > or < ) between the numbers.**

4.   40 ⬭ 50       5.   15 ⬭ 12

6.   22 ⬭ 24       7.   27 ⬭ 17

**Place the two numbers on the correct lines to make the statement correct.**

8.   49      36      _____ > _____

9.   32      23      _____ > _____

10.   12      21      _____ < _____

| Started: | Finished: | Total Time: | Completed: | Correct: |
|---|---|---|---|---|

Name _____  Date _____

**Use the correct symbol ( >, < , or = ) for each group of stars.**

1. ☆ ☆ ☆ ☆ ☆  ⬭  ☆ ☆ ☆ ☆ ☆ ☆ ☆

2. ☆ ☆ ☆ ☆
   ☆ ☆ ☆ ☆  ⬭  ☆ ☆ ☆
               ☆ ☆ ☆

3. ☆ ☆ ☆ ☆ ☆
   ☆ ☆ ☆ ☆ ☆  ⬭  ☆ ☆ ☆ ☆ ☆
                 ☆ ☆ ☆ ☆ ☆

4. ☆ ☆ ☆ ☆ ☆
   ☆ ☆ ☆ ☆  ⬭  ☆ ☆ ☆
              ☆ ☆ ☆

**Use the correct symbol ( > , < , or = ) for each pair of numbers.**

5.  16  ⬭  18        6.  8  ⬭  5

7.  50  ⬭  50        8.  62  ⬭  76

**Write your own *greater than* sentence.**

9. 15 > _____

**Write your own *less than* sentence.**

10. 15 < _____

| Started: | Finished: | Total Time: | Completed: | Correct: |
|---|---|---|---|---|

Name _____  Date _____

**Use the words in the word box to name each symbol.**

| greater than | less than | equal to |
| --- | --- | --- |

1. > _____

2. = _____

3. < _____

**Choose the correct number from each box to complete the sentences.**

4. 25 >  | 24 | _____
         | 26 |

5. 27 <  | 28 | _____
         | 26 |

6. 30 >  | 29 | _____
         | 31 |

7. 43 <  | 44 | _____
         | 42 |

**Use the three numbers in the box to write three sentences using the symbols ( > , < , or = ).  There is more than one possible answer.**

| 3 | 13 | 30 |
| --- | --- | --- |

8. _____ > _____

9. _____ < _____

10. _____ = _____

Name _____    Date _____

## Answer the questions about the number line.

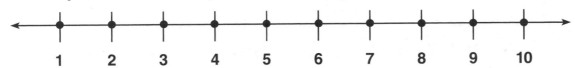

1   2   3   4   5   6   7   8   9   10

**1.** Circle the *odd* numbers under the number line.

**2.** Underline the *even* numbers under the number line.

**3.** Which number is 2 *more than* 8? _____

**4.** Which number is 4 *less than* 7? _____

## Use the number line to solve each problem.

1   2   3   4   5   6   7   8   9   10

**5.** $3 + 5 =$ _____

**6.** $5 + 2 =$ _____

**7.** $10 - 6 =$ _____

**8.** $9 - 7 =$ _____

## Use the number line to solve the riddles.

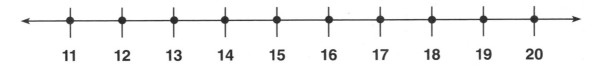

11   12   13   14   15   16   17   18   19   20

**9.** This number is more than 11. It is odd. It is greater than 17. It is _____.

**10.** This number is an odd number. It is more than 10 and less than 20. It is 4 less than a number that ends in 5.

It is _____.

| Started: | Finished: | Total Time: | Completed: | Correct: |
|---|---|---|---|---|

Name _____ Date _____

**Use the number line to answer questions 1–5.**

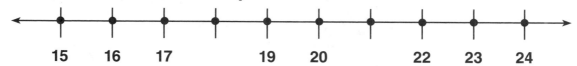

**1.** Add the two missing numbers to the number line.

**2.** What is the first number on the number line? _____

**3.** What is the last number on the number line? _____

**4.** What number is two less than the last number? _____

**5.** What number is three more than the first number? _____

**Answer questions 6 – 8.  Use the number line.**

**6.** Add the two missing numbers to the number line.

**7.** Use the number line to count 5 more than 9.
What number did you land on? _____

**8.** Use the number line to count 6 less than 16.
What number did you land on? _____

**Use the number line to solve the riddles.**

**9.** This number is even.  It has a 1 in the
tens place and an 8 in the ones place.  It is _____.

**10.** This number is an odd number.  It is more than 10 and
less than 20.  It is 5 less than a number that ends in 8.  It is _____.

| Started: | Finished: | Total Time: | Completed: | Correct: |
|---|---|---|---|---|

Name _____      Date _____

## Use the number line to help you solve each problem.

```
0  1  2  3  4  5  6  7  8  9  10  11  12  13  14  15  16  17  18  19  20
```

**1.** 9 + 4 = _____

**2.** 7 + 7 = _____

**3.** 20 – 8 = _____

**4.** 15 – 7 = _____

## Do the math. Find the numbers on the number line.

```
0  1  2  3  4  5  6  7  8  9  10  11  12  13  14  15  16  17  18  19  20
```

**5.** This number is 7 less than 10. It is _____.

**6.** This number is 5 more than 1. It is _____.

**7.** This number is 5 less than 20. It is _____.

**8.** This number is 9 more than 11. It is _____.

## Use the number line to solve the riddles.

```
0  1  2  3  4  5  6  7  8  9  10  11  12  13  14  15  16  17  18  19  20
```

**9.** This number is less than 20 and more than 0. It has a 0 in the ones place.

It is _____.

**10.** This number is an odd number. It is more than 10 and less than 20.
It is 4 more than a number that ends in 5.

It is _____.

| Started: | Finished: | Total Time: | Completed: | Correct: |
|----------|-----------|-------------|------------|----------|

Name _____ Date _____

## Find the sums.

1. ☺☺☺☺☺ + ☺☺☺ = _____

2. ☺☺☺☺ + ☺☺☺☺☺☺ = _____

3. ☺☺☺ + ☺☺☺ + ☺☺☺ = _____

4. ☺☺☺☺☺☺ + ☺☺☺☺☺☺ = _____

## Add the stars.

| 5. ☆☆☆☆☆ + ☆☆ = _____ | 6. ☆☆☆ + ☆☆☆☆☆☆ = _____ |
|---|---|
| 7. ☆☆☆☆☆☆ + ☆☆☆ = _____ | 8. ☆☆☆☆☆ + ☆☆☆☆☆☆ = _____ |

## Solve the word problems. Show your work.

9. Jett has 4 eggs and Noah has 5 eggs. How many eggs do they have altogether?

_____ eggs

10. Sara has 6 eggs and Erica has 3 eggs. How many eggs do they have altogether?

_____ eggs

| Started: | Finished: | Total Time: | Completed: | Correct: |
|---|---|---|---|---|

# Addition

Name _____ Date _____

## Add to find each sum.

**1.** $3 + 2 =$ _____

**2.** $2 + 2 =$ _____

**3.** $4 + 1 =$ _____

**4.** $5 + 0 =$ _____

## Count each set.  Write the problem to find the sum.

**5.** ▲▲▲▲ + ▲▲▲ = _____

**6.** ■■■■ + ■ = _____

**7.** ⬠⬠ + ⬠⬠ = _____

## Solve the word problems.  Show your work.

| **8.** | Lydia has 2 puppies and Zeke has 3 puppies. How many puppies do they have altogether? |
|---|---|
| | _____ + _____ = _____ **puppies** |
| **9.** | Tom had 2 pencils.  His mom gave him 2 new pencils. How many pencils does he have now? |
| | _____ + _____ = _____ **pencils** |
| **10.** | Dad ate 2 cookies and Sam ate 1 cookie. How many cookies did they eat altogether? |
| | _____ + _____ = _____ **cookies** |

| Started: | Finished: | Total Time: | Completed: | Correct: |
|---|---|---|---|---|

Name _____    Date _____

## Count each set.  Write the problem and find the sum.

1. ⚽⚽⚽⚽⚽ + ⚽⚽ = _____

2. ⚾⚾⚾⚾⚾ + ⚾⚾⚾⚾ = _____

3. 🏀🏀🏀🏀 + 🏀🏀 = _____

4. 🏈🏈🏈 + 🏈🏈🏈🏈🏈🏈 = _____

## Add each problem.

| 5. | 4 | 6. | 5 | 7. | 2 | 8. | 1 |
|----|---|----|---|----|---|----|---|
|    | + 3 |  | + 4 |  | + 6 |  | + 9 |

## Solve the word problems.  Show your work.

| 9. | There were 5 chicks in the nest and 3 in the yard.  How many chicks were there altogether? |
|----|------|
|    | _____ + _____ = _____ **chicks** |
| 10. | Lee saw 4 bunnies on his way to school and 6 bunnies on his way home.  How many bunnies did he see? |
|    | _____ + _____ = _____ **bunnies** |

| Started: | Finished: | Total Time: | Completed: | Correct: |
|----------|-----------|-------------|------------|----------|

Name _____ Date _____

## Add each problem.

1.    7
   + 3

2.    2
   + 8

## Find the missing numbers.

3. $4 + 3 =$ _____ and _____ $+ 4 = 7$

4. $7 + 3 =$ _____ and $3 +$ _____ $= 10$

5. $5 + 4 =$ _____ and _____ $+ 5 = 9$

6. $6 + 2 =$ _____ and $2 +$ _____ $= 8$

## Answer *True* or *False*.

7. $5 + 3 = 3 + 5$     **True**     **False**

8. $2 + 3 = 4 + 2$     **True**     **False**

9. $5 + 5 = 3 + 7$     **True**     **False**

## Draw circles to show sets. Solve the problem.

10.

$8 + 2 =$ _____

| Started: | Finished: | Total Time: | Completed: | Correct: |
| --- | --- | --- | --- | --- |

Name _____  Date _____

## Answer *True* or *False*.

**1.** $4 + 4 = 1 + 6$    **True**    **False**

**2.** $3 + 4 = 2 + 5$    **True**    **False**

**3.** $8 + 1 = 3 + 6$    **True**    **False**

## Add the doubles.

**4.**   5
  + 5

**5.**   4
  + 4

**6.** $2 + 2 =$ _____

**7.** $3 + 3 =$ _____

## Solve the word problems.  Show your work.

| 8. | Blake had 4 cars.  Jake had 6 cars. How many cars did they have altogether? |
|----|------|
|  | _____ + _____ = _____ **cars** |
| 9. | Nina has 4 shirts.  Tina has 5 shirts. How many shirts do the girls have? |
|  | _____ + _____ = _____ **shirts** |
| 10. | Finn has 5 crayons and Linn has 5 crayons. How many crayons do they have? |
|  | _____ + _____ = _____ **crayons** |

| Started: | Finished: | Total Time: | Completed: | Correct: |
|----------|-----------|-------------|------------|----------|

Name _____ Date _____

## Fill in the missing number to make 10.

**1.** 5 + _____ = 10

**2.** 4 + _____ = 10

**3.** 3 + _____ = 10

**4.** 2 + _____ = 10

**5.** 1 + _____ = 10

## Add three numbers to solve.

**6.**    2
       3
   + 3

**7.**    5
       3
   + 1

**8.**    4
       4
   + 1

## Solve the word problems.  Count by 2s.  Show your work.

**9.** | Sam has 4 pairs of mittens.  How many mittens does Sam have?

_____ + _____ + _____ + _____ = _____ **mittens**

**10.** | Dan has 6 pairs of boots.  How many boots does Dan have?

_____ + _____ + _____ + _____ + _____ + _____ = _____ **boots**

| Started: | Finished: | Total Time: | Completed: | Correct: |

Name _____ Date _____

## Add each group of objects to 10. Find the sum.

**1.** $10 +$ ⬡⬡⬡ = _____

**2.** $10 +$ ⬡⬡⬡⬡⬡ = _____

**3.** $10 +$ ⬡⬡ = _____

**4.** $10 +$ ⬡⬡⬡⬡ = _____

## Find the sums.

**5.**    10
    $+\ 5$

**6.**    10
    $+\ 3$

**7.**    10
    $+\ 4$

## What are three ways to make 15?

**8.** $9 +$ _____ $= 15$

**9.** _____ $+ 5 = 15$

**10.** $8 +$ _____ $= 15$

| Started: | Finished: | Total Time: | Completed: | Correct: |
|---|---|---|---|---|

Name _____  Date _____

**Add each group of objects to 10.  Find the sum.**

1. 10 + ⬡⬡⬡⬡⬡⬡ = _____

2. 10 + ⬡⬡⬡⬡⬡⬡⬡⬡ = _____

3. 10 + ⬡⬡⬡⬡⬡⬡⬡ = _____

4. 10 + ⬡⬡⬡⬡⬡⬡⬡⬡ = _____

**Find the sums.**

| 5. | 10 | 6. | 10 | 7. | 10 |
|----|----|----|----|----|----|
|    | + 9 |   | + 6 |   | + 7 |

**Fill in the blanks to solve each problem.  Remember, 10 + 10 = 20.**

8. 10 + _____ + 6 = 20

9. 10 + 5 + _____ = 20

10. 10 + _____ + 2 = 20

| Started: | Finished: | Total Time: | Completed: | Correct: |
|----------|-----------|-------------|------------|----------|

Name _____ Date _____

**Fill in the blanks in each number pattern.**

**1.** 2, _____, 6, _____, 10, _____, 14, _____, _____, 20

**2.** 5, _____, 15, _____, 25, _____, 35, _____, 45, _____

**3.** 3, _____, 9, _____, 15, _____, 21, _____, 27, _____

**Add three numbers to solve. First circle the 2 numbers that equal 10.**

**4.**    5
          6
       +  5
       _____

**5.**    8
          2
       +  7
       _____

**6.**    6
          9
       +  4
       _____

**7.**    7
          3
       +  3
       _____

**Solve the doubles.**

**8.** 8 + 8 = _____

**9.** 7 + 7 = _____

**10.** 9 + 9 = _____

| Started: | Finished: | Total Time: | Completed: | Correct: |
|----------|-----------|-------------|------------|----------|

Name _____ Date _____

**Finish adding shapes to create sets to solve each problem.**

1.  9
   + 8

2.  5
   + 7

3.  8
   + 6

4.  4
   + 9

**Add and solve.**

5.    6        6.    8        7.    4        8.    7
    + 9           + 6           + 8           + 9

**Solve the word problems.  Show your work.**

9. There are 6 red bikes and 9 black bikes at school.
   How many bikes are there altogether?

   _____ + _____ = _____ **bikes**

10. Bruce counted 9 green trucks and 9 white trucks on the street.
    How many trucks did he see?

    _____ + _____ = _____ **trucks**

| Started: | Finished: | Total Time: | Completed: | Correct: |
|----------|-----------|-------------|------------|----------|

# Addition

Name _____  Date _____

## Find the sums.

1.  14
   + 5

2.  31
   + 6

3.  14
   + 4

4.  56
   + 3

5.  26
   + 2

6.  13
   + 5

## Count by 5s to solve each problem.

**7.** 5 + 5 + 5 + 5 + 5 + 5 + 5 + 5 + 5 + 5 + 5 = _____

**8.** 5 + 5 + 5 + 5 + 5 + 5 + 5 + 5 + 5 + 5 + 5 + 5 + 5 + 5 + 5 = _____

## Solve the word problems.  Show your work.

| 9. | There are 22 trees in our backyard and 7 trees in the front yard. How many trees are there altogether? |
|---|---|
| | _____ trees |

| 10. | Leah has read 42 pages.  She had to read 6 more to finish the book.  How many pages long is the book? |
|---|---|
| | _____ pages |

| Started: | Finished: | Total Time: | Completed: | Correct: |
|---|---|---|---|---|

Name _____ Date _____

## Find the sums. First add the ones column and then add the 10s column.

1.  23
    + 16

2.  41
    +  7

3.  64
    + 33

4.  62
    +  6

5.  72
    +  7

6.  50
    + 34

## Count by 10s to solve each problem.

**7.** 10 + 10 + 10 + 10 + 10 + 10 + 10 = _____

**8.** 10 + 10 + 10 + 10 + 10 + 10 + 10 + 10 + 10 + 10 = _____

## Solve the word problems. Show your work.

| 9. | Siena put 20 cookies on the plate. Terra added 8 cookies. How many cookies are on the plate now? |
| --- | --- |

+ _____

_____ **cookies**

| 10. | Rosa had 6 pets and Joe had 5 pets. Then, they got 2 birds. How many pets do they have altogether? |
| --- | --- |

+ _____

_____ **pets**

| Started: | Finished: | Total Time: | Completed: | Correct: |
| --- | --- | --- | --- | --- |

46 ©Teacher Created Resources

Name _____  Date _____

**Cross out the insects to subtract. Write each problem and solve.**

| 1. Cross out 5 and subtract. | 2. Cross out 7 and subtract. |
|---|---|
|  |  |
| _____ – _____ = _____ | _____ – _____ = _____ |
| 3. Cross out 3 and subtract. | 4. Cross out 4 and subtract. |
|  | 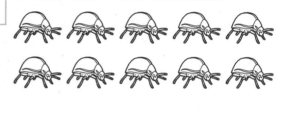 |
| _____ – _____ = _____ | _____ – _____ = _____ |

**Subtract.**

**5.** $7 - 4 =$ _____

**6.** $10 - 5 =$ _____

**7.** $8 - 6 =$ _____

**8.** $9 - 3 =$ _____

**Solve the word problems. Show your work.**

| 9. | Kyle had 10 hats in May. He only had 3 hats by July. How many hats did he lose? |
|---|---|
| | _____ – _____ = _____ **hats** |
| 10. | Lily had 9 hats for her party. She used 7. How many hats does she have left? |
| | _____ – _____ = _____ **hats** |

| Started: | Finished: | Total Time: | Completed: | Correct: |
|---|---|---|---|---|

# Subtraction

Name _____  Date _____

**Solve the subtraction problems.**

**1.** $14 - 8 =$ _____

**2.** $13 - 9 =$ _____

**Find the difference for each problem.**

**3.**    7
      − 3
      ☐

**4.**    8
      − 8
      ☐

**5.**    2
      − 1
      ☐

**6.**    9
      − 6
      ☐

**7.**    4
      − 4
      ☐

**8.**    5
      − 3
      ☐

**Solve the word problems.  Show your work.**

| 9. | There were 9 balloons on the grass.  Then 3 popped! How many balloons were left? |
|---|---|
| | _____ − _____ = _____ **balloons** |
| 10. | Bob was holding 12 balloons.  The wind blew 7 away. How many balloons did he have left? |
| | _____ − _____ = _____ **balloons** |

| Started: | Finished: | Total Time: | Completed: | Correct: |
|---|---|---|---|---|

Name _____  Date _____

## Find the difference.

1.   10
   − 8

2.    9
    − 4

## Solve the subtraction problems.

3. 15 − 7 = _____

4. 12 − 8 = _____

## Fill in the missing numbers to solve.

5.    10
    − 4
    ☐

6.    14
    − ☐
      7

7.    12
    − ☐
      6

8.    16
    − ☐
      9

## Answer *True* or *False*.

9. 15 − 7 = 8          **True     False**

10. 13 − 8 = 10          **True     False**

| Started: | Finished: | Total Time: | Completed: | Correct: |
|----------|-----------|-------------|------------|----------|

# Subtraction

Name _____  Date _____

## Find the differences.

**1.**  15
     − 7

**2.**  11
     − 6

**3.**  13
     − 9

## Solve the subtraction problems.

**4.** 13 − 7 = _____

**5.** 12 − 5 = _____

**6.** 14 − 9 = _____

## Find the missing numbers.

**7.** 15 − _____ = 6

**8.** 13 − _____ = 4

## Solve the word problems.  Show your work.

| | |
|---|---|
| **9.** | Tad had 12 eggs.  He gave 6 to his mom.  How many eggs did he have left? <br><br> _____ − _____ = _____ **eggs** |
| **10.** | Brad had 10 eggs.  He ate 3 eggs.  How many eggs did he have left? <br><br> _____ − _____ = _____ **eggs** |

| Started: | Finished: | Total Time: | Completed: | Correct: |
|---|---|---|---|---|

# Subtraction

Name _____ Date _____

**Cross out the stars to subtract. Write each problem and solve.**

**1.** Cross out 5 and subtract.

_____ – _____ = _____

**2.** Cross out 3 and subtract.

_____ – _____ = _____

**3.** Cross out 7 and subtract.

_____ – _____ = _____

**4.** Cross out 4 and subtract.

_____ – _____ = _____

**Subtract.**

**5.** $14 - 4 =$ _____

**6.** $20 - 10 =$ _____

**7.** $18 - 9 =$ _____

**8.** $16 - 8 =$ _____

**9.** $11 -$ _____ $= 2$

**10.** $14 -$ _____ $= 5$

| Started: | Finished: | Total Time: | Completed: | Correct: |
|---|---|---|---|---|

Name _____    Date _____

**Use the numbers in each box to make 2 subtraction problems.**

| 9 | 4 | 5 |

1. _____ – _____ = _____     2. _____ – _____ = _____

| 7 | 10 | 3 |

3. _____ – _____ = _____     4. _____ – _____ = _____

**Answer *True* or *False*.**

5. $10 - 5 = 6$         **True**     **False**

6. $12 - 7 = 5$         **True**     **False**

7. $15 - 8 = 6$         **True**     **False**

8. $14 - 8 = 6$         **True**     **False**

**Solve the word problems. Show your work.**

| 9. | Nancy had 14 grapes. She ate 8 grapes. How many did she have left? |
|---|---|
| | _____ – _____ = _____ **grapes** |
| 10. | John had 15 grapes. He ate 11 grapes. How many did he have left? |
| | _____ – _____ = _____ **grapes** |

| Started: | Finished: | Total Time: | Completed: | Correct: |

Name _____  Date _____

## Cross out the stars to subtract. Write each problem and solve.

| 1. Cross out 7 and subtract. | 2. Cross out 9 and subtract. |
|---|---|

_____ – _____ = _____     _____ – _____ = _____

## Find the differences.

3. $17 - 8 =$ _____

4. $18 - 8 =$ _____

5. $\begin{array}{r} 19 \\ -\,10 \\ \hline \end{array}$

6. $\begin{array}{r} 16 \\ -\,\ 7 \\ \hline \end{array}$

## Use the numbers in each box to make 2 subtraction problems.

| 10 | 4 | 6 |
|---|---|---|

7. _____ – _____ = _____

8. _____ – _____ = _____

| 5 | 13 | 8 |
|---|---|---|

9. _____ – _____ = _____

10. _____ – _____ = _____

| Started: | Finished: | Total Time: | Completed: | Correct: |
|---|---|---|---|---|

# Subtraction

Name _____ Date _____

## Choose the correct answer. Fill in the missing numbers.

1. _____ − 4 = 7

( 11 )    ( 12 )

2. _____ − 6 = 9

( 14 )    ( 15 )

3. _____ − 7 = 8

( 15 )    ( 16 )

4. _____ − 7 = 6

( 17 )    ( 13 )

## Cross out the stars and subtract. Write each problem and solve.

| 5. | Cross out 9 and subtract. | 6. | Cross out 7 and subtract. |
|---|---|---|---|

_____ − _____ = _____

_____ − _____ = _____

## Use the numbers in each box to make 2 subtraction problems.

```
12      4      8
```

7. _____ − _____ = _____

8. _____ − _____ = _____

```
9      13      4
```

9. _____ − _____ = _____

10. _____ − _____ = _____

| Started: | Finished: | Total Time: | Completed: | Correct: |
|---|---|---|---|---|

Name _____ Date _____

**Use the numbers in each box to make 2 subtraction problems.**

4          11          7

1. _____ – _____ = _____          2. _____ – _____ = _____

7          15          8

3. _____ – _____ = _____          4. _____ – _____ = _____

**Answer *True* or *False*.**

**5.** $16 - 8 = 8$          **True          False**

**6.** $15 - 10 = 8$          **True          False**

**7.** $14 - 8 = 6$          **True          False**

**8.** $13 - 9 = 4$          **True          False**

**Circle the correct answer and fill in the blank.**

**9.** $13 - 7 =$ _____          **5          6          7**

**10.** $17 - 9 =$ _____          **7          8          9**

| Started: | Finished: | Total Time: | Completed: | Correct: |
|----------|-----------|-------------|------------|----------|

# Subtraction

Name _____ Date _____

**Choose the correct answer for each problem.  Fill in the missing numbers.**

1. _____ − 6 = 6

   (12)    (10)

2. _____ − 7 = 7

   (13)    (14)

3. _____ − 10 = 10

   (20)    (10)

4. _____ − 9 = 9

   (19)    (18)

**Use the numbers in each box to make 2 subtraction problems.**

| 19 | 9 | 10 |
|----|---|----|

5. _____ − _____ = _____

6. _____ − _____ = _____

| 9 | 17 | 8 |
|---|----|---|

7. _____ − _____ = _____

8. _____ − _____ = _____

**Solve the word problems.  Show your work.**

| 9. | Cal's book has 19 pages.  He has read 16 pages. How many pages does he have left to read? |
|----|----|
|    | − _____ |
|    | _____ **pages** |
| 10. | There were 16 books on the desk.  The teacher took 8 books. How many books were left? |
|    | − _____ |
|    | _____ **books** |

| Started: | Finished: | Total Time: | Completed: | Correct: |
|----------|-----------|-------------|------------|----------|

Name _____ Date _____

## Use the numbers in each box to make 2 subtraction problems.

| 18      15      3 |

1. _____ – _____ = _____      2. _____ – _____ = _____

| 7      16      9 |

3. _____ – _____ = _____      4. _____ – _____ = _____

## Find the difference.

5.
```
   17
 –  6
─────
```

6.
```
   20
 – 10
─────
```

7.
```
   15
 –  8
─────
```

8.
```
   17
 –  9
─────
```

## Solve the word problems.  Show your work.

| 9. | There were 20 students on the bus.  Ten students got off. How many students were still on the bus? |
|---|---|
| | _____ students |

| 10. | There are 18 students in the class.  Only 12 students did their reading.  How many students still need to read? |
|---|---|
| | _____ students |

| Started: | Finished: | Total Time: | Completed: | Correct: |

Name _____     Date _____

## Fill in the missing numbers.

1. ☐ − 6 = 6

2. ☐ − 8 = 8

3. ☐ − 7 = 7

4. ☐ − 10 = 10

## Answer *True* or *False*.

5. 18 − 9 = 9     **True**     **False**

6. 20 − 10 = 8     **True**     **False**

7. 18 − 8 = 10     **True**     **False**

8. 16 − 7 = 9     **True**     **False**

## Solve the word problems. Show your work.

| 9. | Colton's team has 14 players. Only 7 can play at a time. How many players have to sit out? |
|---|---|

_____ **players**

−_____

| 10. | Shelley's team has 16 players. Five players missed the game. How many players were at the game? |
|---|---|

_____ **players**

−_____

| Started: | Finished: | Total Time: | Completed: | Correct: |
|---|---|---|---|---|

Name _____     Date _____

## Solve the addition problems.

**1.** 6 + 2 = ☐                    **2.** 4 + 3 = ☐

## Solve the subtraction problems.

**3.** 6 − 2 = ☐                    **4.** 8 − 4 = ☐

## Solve the problems.

**5.** 7 + 3 = ☐                    **6.** 3 + 7 = ☐

**7.** 10 − 3 = ☐                   **8.** 10 − 7 = ☐

## Solve the word problems.  Circle the operation you used.

| 9. | Ella has 3 dolls.  Bella has 4 dolls. How many dolls do they have altogether?  **Addition**          **Subtraction** |
|---|---|
| 10. | Cam has 5 soccer balls.  Sam has 2 soccer balls. How many more soccer balls does Cam have?  **Addition**          **Subtraction** |

| Started: | Finished: | Total Time: | Completed: | Correct: |
|---|---|---|---|---|

Name _____ Date _____

## Solve the addition problems.

**1.**    5
   + 5
   ‾‾‾

**2.**    3
   + 6
   ‾‾‾

## Solve the subtraction problems.

**3.**   10
   – 3
   ‾‾‾

**4.**    7
   – 5
   ‾‾‾

## Solve the problems.

**5.**    2
   + 8
   ‾‾‾

**6.**   10
   – 2
   ‾‾‾

**7.**    8
   + 2
   ‾‾‾

**8.**   10
   – 8
   ‾‾‾

## Solve the problems.

**9.** Add two more triangles. What is the total?

 +

_____ + _____ = _____

**10.** Cross out six squares. How many squares are left?

_____ – _____ = _____

| Started: | Finished: | Total Time: | Completed: | Correct: |
|---|---|---|---|---|

Name _____ Date _____

## Solve the addition problems.

**1.** $6 + 9 = \boxed{\phantom{00}}$

**2.** $8 + 3 = \boxed{\phantom{00}}$

## Solve the subtraction problems.

**3.** $14 - 7 = \boxed{\phantom{00}}$

**4.** $17 - 8 = \boxed{\phantom{00}}$

## Solve the problems.

**5.** $6 + 7 = \boxed{\phantom{00}}$

**6.** $7 + 6 = \boxed{\phantom{00}}$

**7.** $13 - 7 = \boxed{\phantom{00}}$

**8.** $13 - 6 = \boxed{\phantom{00}}$

## Solve the word problems. Circle the operation you used.

| 9. | Brandon has 12 cards. Marco has 9 cards. How many more cards does Brandon have? |
|---|---|
| | **Addition**       **Subtraction** |
| 10. | There are 8 cookies on one plate and 7 cookies on another plate. How many cookies are there altogether? |
| | **Addition**       **Subtraction** |

| Started: | Finished: | Total Time: | Completed: | Correct: |
|---|---|---|---|---|

Name _____ Date _____

## Solve the addition problems.

| **1.** | 10 | **2.** | 8 | **3.** | 4 |
|---|---|---|---|---|---|
| | + 5 | | + 6 | | + 8 |

## Solve the subtraction problems.

| **4.** | 13 | **5.** | 12 | **6.** | 15 |
|---|---|---|---|---|---|
| | − 5 | | − 7 | | − 9 |

## Answer *True* or *False*.

**7.** $10 - 6 = 5$          **True**     **False**

**8.** $14 - 8 = 6$          **True**     **False**

**9.** $13 - 7 = 6$          **True**     **False**

## Solve the word problem.  Circle the operation you used.

| **10.** | Serena made 12 cupcakes.  Her family ate 6 cupcakes after dinner. How many cupcakes were left? |
|---|---|
| | |
| | **Addition**          **Subtraction** |

| Started: | Finished: | Total Time: | Completed: | Correct: |
|---|---|---|---|---|

Name _____     Date _____

## Solve the addition problems.

**1.**    12
    + 6

**2.**    11
    + 9

**3.**    14
    + 5

## Solve the subtraction problems.

**4.**    13
    − 5

**5.**    19
    − 7

**6.**    15
    − 9

## Answer *True* or *False*.

**7.** $9 + 9 = 18$      **True**     **False**

**8.** $8 + 7 = 16$      **True**     **False**

## Solve the word problems. Circle the operation you used.

| **9.** | The team scored 7 points in the first game and 9 points in the second game. How many points did they score altogether? |
|---|---|
| | **Addition**      **Subtraction** |
| **10.** | Josh had 16 comic books. He sold 8. How many does he have left? |
| | **Addition**      **Subtraction** |

| Started: | Finished: | Total Time: | Completed: | Correct: |
|---|---|---|---|---|

Name _____    Date _____

## Find the missing numbers to solve the problems.

1. $18 - \boxed{\phantom{0}} = 9$

2. $6 + \boxed{\phantom{0}} = 14$

## Solve the subtraction problems.

3.     17
   $-$   8

4.     16
   $-$   9

## Solve the addition problems.

5.     12
   $+$   5

6.      7
   $+$   9

## Answer *True* or *False*.

7. $20 - 10 = 10$      **True**      **False**

8. $18 - 8 = 10$      **True**      **False**

9. $17 - 8 = 10$      **True**      **False**

## Solve the word problem. Circle the operation you used.

| 10. | Coach had 16 cones. He put 9 cones on the field. How many cones did he have left? |
|---|---|
| | **Addition**           **Subtraction** |

| Started: | Finished: | Total Time: | Completed: | Correct: |
|---|---|---|---|---|

Name _____　　　Date _____

## Look at the pictures to answer the questions.

A. 　　　　　B.

**1.** Which pencil is longer? _____　　**2.** Which pencil is shorter? _____

A. 　　B.

**3.** Which chain is longer? _____　　**4.** Which chain is shorter? _____

## Answer *True* or *False*.

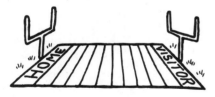　　

**5.** The square beads are shorter.　　**True**　　**False**

**6.** The round beads are shorter.　　**True**　　**False**

## Circle the tool you would use to measure how long a pencil is.

**7. A.**　　　　　　**B.**　　　　　　**C.**

## Circle the best unit of measurement to measure each item.

**8.** 　　　　　inches　　　yards

**9.** 　　　　　feet　　　inches

**10.** 　　　　　inches　　　feet

| Started: | Finished: | Total Time: | Completed: | Correct: |

Name _____ Date _____

**Look at the pictures to answer the questions.  Write A or B on each line.**

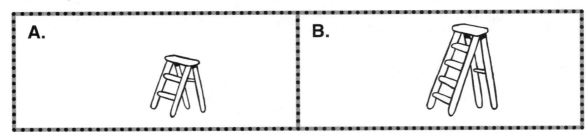

**1.** Which ladder is *shorter*? _____

**2.** Which ladder is *taller*? _____

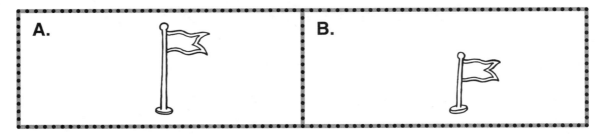

**3.** Which flagpole is *taller*? _____

**4.** Which flagpole is *shorter*? _____

**Follow the directions.**

**5.** Draw a rectangle that is *shorter* than the rectangle to the right.

**6.** Draw a rectangle that is *taller* than the rectangle to the right.

**Circle the item that would be *taller*.**

**7.** a dog house  *or*  a house for people

**8.** a horse  *or*  a dog

**Circle the item that would be *shorter*.**

**9.** an elephant  *or*  a giraffe

**10.** a cat  *or*  a mouse

| Started: | Finished: | Total Time: | Completed: | Correct: |
| --- | --- | --- | --- | --- |

Name _____  Date _____

## Fill in the blanks to answer the questions.

1. The car is _____ than the truck.
   **larger    smaller**

2. The truck is _____ than the car.
   **larger    smaller**

3. The tennis ball is _____ than the basketball.
   **larger       smaller**

4. The basketball is _____ than the tennis ball.
   **larger       smaller**

## Think about it.  Circle your answers.

5. What is *larger*?     an ocean  **or**  a puddle

6. What is *smaller*?     a mountain  **or**  a hill

## Follow the directions.

7. Draw a small square in the middle of the box.

8. Draw a smaller circle in your square.

9. Draw a larger triangle around your square.

10. Which shape is the largest? _____

| Started: | Finished: | Total Time: | Completed: | Correct: |
|----------|-----------|-------------|------------|----------|

Name _____      Date _____

**Read the words in the word box. Use the words to label the clowns.**

1.

2.

3.

| short |
| shorter |
| shortest |

_____      _____      _____

**Read the words in the word box. Use the words to label the trees.**

4.

5.

6.

| tall |
| taller |
| tallest |

_____      _____      _____

**Follow the directions.**

**7.** Circle the tallest man.

**8.** Draw a triangle around the shortest man.

**9.** Cross out the man in the middle.

**Solve the word problem.**

| 10. | Jack made a tower with 10 blocks. Brandon made a tower with 7 blocks. How many more blocks did Jack use? |
|---|---|
| | _____ – _____ = _____ **blocks** |

| Started: | Finished: | Total Time: | Completed: | Correct: |
|---|---|---|---|---|

Name _____　　Date _____

## Read each question and circle your answer.

1. Which weighs *more*, a fish or a feather?　　

2. Which weighs *less*, a tree or a flower?　　

3. Which weighs *more*, a crab or a shark?　　

4. Which weighs *less*, a cat or a cow?　　

## Circle the item in each pair that would be *heavier*.

| 5. | | 6. | |
|----|----|----|----|
|  |  |  |  |

## Circle the item in each pair that would weigh *less*.

7. a boot **or** a slipper

8. a balloon **or** a soccer ball

9. an empty glass **or** a glass of water

10. a book **or** a pencil

| Started: | Finished: | Total Time: | Completed: | Correct: |

Name _____  Date _____

## Circle the tool you would use to measure liquids.

1.  A.   B.   C.

## Each container holds a different amount.  Label each container.

pint        quart        gallon

2.         3.         4.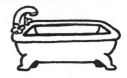

_____     _____     _____

## Circle the correct answer for each question.

A.         B.         C.

5. Which item holds the *least* liquid?        A       B       C

6. Which item holds the *most* liquid?         A       B       C

## Answer *True* or *False*.

7. A coffee cup holds more than a gallon.        **True**        **False**

8. A swimming pool holds more than a gallon.        **True**        **False**

9. A pint of water would fill a bathtub.        **True**        **False**

10. A quart of milk is more than a pint of milk.        **True**        **False**

| Started: | Finished: | Total Time: | Completed: | Correct: |
|----------|-----------|-------------|------------|----------|

Name _____  Date _____

**Use the thermometers to answer questions 1–5. Write the correct letter for each answer.**

**A.    B.    C.**

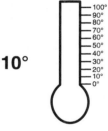

1. Which thermometer shows 30°? _____

2. Which thermometer shows 20°? _____

3. Which thermometer shows 90°? _____

4. Which shows the coldest temperature? _____

5. Which shows the hottest temperature? _____

**Fill in the thermometers to show the correct temperatures.**

6. **40°**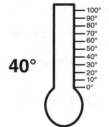

7. **100°**

8. **10°**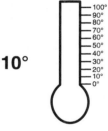

**Think about the weather. Then follow the directions for 9 and 10.**

9. Circle items of clothing you might wear if it was hot outside.

10. Circle items of clothing you might wear if it was cold outside.

| Started: | Finished: | Total Time: | Completed: | Correct: |
|---|---|---|---|---|

Name _____     Date _____

## Circle your answers.

**1.** About how many paperclips long is the paintbrush?    **2**   **3**   **4**   **5**   **6**

**2.** How many paperclips long would two paintbrushes be?   **4**   **5**   **6**   **7**   **8**

_____ + _____ = _____

## Answer the questions about the lines.

**3.** Which line is the *shortest*? _____

**4.** Which line is the *longest*? _____

**A.** ▬▬▬▬▬▬▬▬

**B.** ▬▬▬▬▬▬▬▬▬▬

**C.** ▬▬▬▬▬▬▬

## Each watering can is a different size. Answer the questions for 5–7.

**5.** Circle the watering can that is *large*.

**6.** Cross out the watering can that is *medium*.

**7.** Draw a box around the one that is *small*.

## Circle the letter of the item in each row that would weigh the *least*.

**8.**   **A.**       **B.**

**9.**   **A.**       **B.**

**10.** **A.**       **B.**

| Started: | Finished: | Total Time: | Completed: | Correct: |
|---|---|---|---|---|
| | | | | |

Name _____  Date _____

**Answer the questions about measuring tools.  Write the correct letter for each answer.**

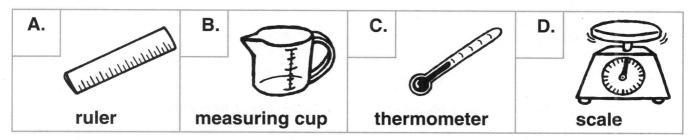

| **A.** ruler | **B.** measuring cup | **C.** thermometer | **D.** scale |

1. This item measures temperature. _____

2. This item measures how long something is. _____

3. This item measures how much something weighs. _____

4. This item measures liquids. _____

**What would be *heavier*?  Circle your answers.**

5. a bike  *or*  a skateboard

6. a book  *or*  a desk

7. a watermelon  *or*  an apple

8. a crayon  *or*  a backpack

**Compare the chains and follow the directions.**

9. Circle the *shortest* chain.

10. Cross out the *longest* chain.

| Started: | Finished: | Total Time: | Completed: | Correct: |

Name _____     Date _____

## Which is a longer period of time? Circle your answers.

**1.** an hour *or* a day

**2.** a month *or* a week

**3.** a year *or* a month

## Which tool would you use to tell time? Circle your answers.

| **4.** | **A.**  | **B.**  |
|---|---|---|
| **5.** | **A.**  | **B.**  |

## Circle the answer to each question.

**6.** How many minutes are in an hour?

    **A.**   30        **B.**   60

**7.** How many hours are in a day?

    **A.**   24        **B.**   12

**8.** Look at the clock. What time is it?

    **A.** 12:00        **B.** 3:00

**9.** Soccer practice starts at 5:00 and lasts for one hour. What time does soccer practice end?

    **A.**   5:00        **B.**   6:00

**10.** Lunch starts at 12:00 and lasts for one hour. What time does lunch end?

    **A.**   1:00        **B.**   11:00

| Started: | Finished: | Total Time: | Completed: | Correct: |
|---|---|---|---|---|

Name _____    Date _____

## Choose the correct time.  Write *A* or *B* on the line.

1.  _____    **A.** 12:00     **B.** 2:00

2.  _____    **A.** 1:00     **B.** 2:00

3.  _____    **A.** 9:00     **B.** 10:00

4.  _____    **A.** 8:00     **B.** 7:00

5.  _____    **A.** 6:00     **B.** 5:00

6.  _____    **A.** 12:00     **B.** 11:00

## Answer *True* or *False*.

7. **Noon** and **12:00** can mean the same time.     **True**       **False**

8. **Midnight** and **12:00** can mean the same time.     **True**       **False**

## Draw hands to show the times on the clocks.

9.    4:00   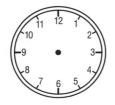     **10.**    10:00  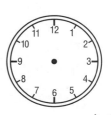

| Started: | Finished: | Total Time: | Completed: | Correct: |
|---|---|---|---|---|

Name _____ Date _____

## Match the times. Write the correct letter next to the analog clock.

**1.**  _____

**2.**  _____

**3.**  _____

**4.**  _____

**5.**  _____

**6.**  _____

**7.**  _____

**8.**  _____

**9.** _____

**10.** _____

**A.** 1:00

**B.** 6:00

**C.** 3:00

**D.** 4:00

**E.** 7:00

**F.** 11:00

**G.** 9:00

**H.** 2:00

**I.** 5:00

**J.** 8:00

| Started: | Finished: | Total Time: | Completed: | Correct: |
|---|---|---|---|---|

Name _____  Date _____

## Fill in each digital clock to match the analog clock.

**1.**

**2.**

**3.**

**4.**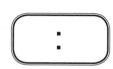

**5.**

**6.**

**7.**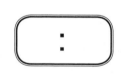

**8.**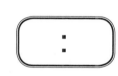

**9.**

**10.**

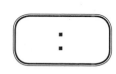
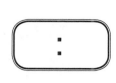
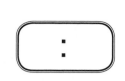

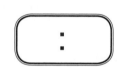

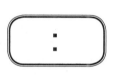

| Started: | Finished: | Total Time: | Completed: | Correct: |
|---|---|---|---|---|

Name _____    Date _____

## Match the times. Write the correct letter next to the analog clock.

1.  _____

2.  _____

3.  _____

4.  _____

5.  _____

6.  _____

7.  _____

8.  _____

9.  _____

10.  _____

A. 8:30

B. 6:30

C. 3:30

D. 1:30

E. 7:30

F. 10:30

G. 9:30

H. 2:30

I. 5:30

J. 4:30

| Started: | Finished: | Total Time: | Completed: | Correct: |
|---|---|---|---|---|

Name _____  Date _____

## Draw hands to show the times on the clocks.

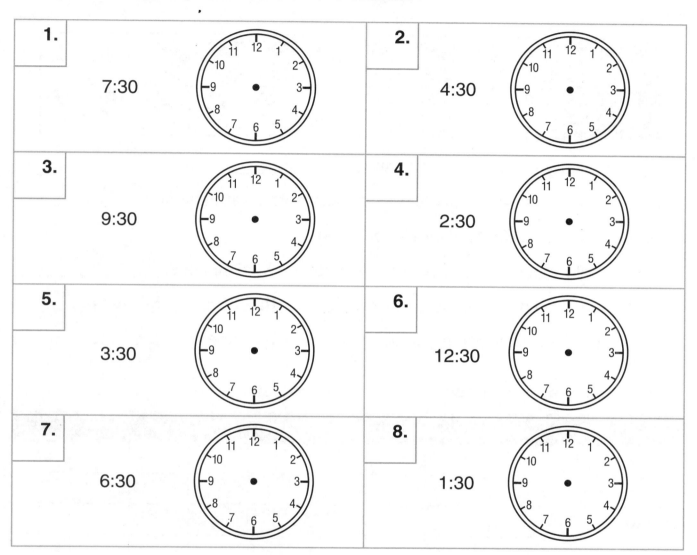

**1.** 7:30

**2.** 4:30

**3.** 9:30

**4.** 2:30

**5.** 3:30

**6.** 12:30

**7.** 6:30

**8.** 1:30

## Circle the correct answer for each question.

**9.** Which letters mean "before midday"?    **A.** a.m.    **B.** p.m.

**10.** Which letters mean "after midday"?    **A.** a.m.    **B.** p.m.

| Started: | Finished: | Total Time: | Completed: | Correct: |
|---|---|---|---|---|

Name _____ Date _____

**Answer the questions below. Each shoe in the pictograph equals one student.**

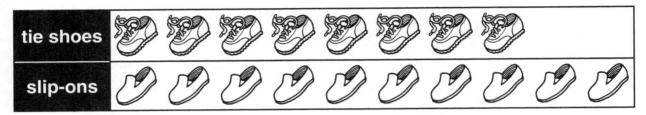

| tie shoes | |
| slip-ons | |

1. How many students wear tie shoes? _____

2. Use tally marks to show how many students wear tie shoes. _____

3. How many students wear slip-on shoes? _____

4. Use tally marks to show how many students wear slip-ons. _____

5. Which shoe do *more* students wear?　　**tie shoes　　slip-ons**

6. Which shoe do *fewer* students wear?　　**tie shoes　　slip-ons**

**Use the bar graph to answer the questions below.**

| Student Hair Color | | | | | | | | | | |
|---|---|---|---|---|---|---|---|---|---|---|
| **Black** | | | | | | | | | | |
| **Brown** | | | | | | | | | | |
| **Blond** | | | | | | | | | | |
| **Red** | | | | | | | | | | |
| | 1 | 2 | 3 | 4 | 5 | 6 | 7 | 8 | 9 | 10 |

7. How many students have black hair? _____

8. How many students have brown hair? _____

9. How many students have blond hair? _____

10. How many students have red hair? _____

| Started: | Finished: | Total Time: | Completed: | Correct: |
|---|---|---|---|---|

Name _____ Date _____

**Use the pictograph to answer the questions below. Each ball equals one vote.**

| Favorite Sport | | | | | | | | | | |
|---|---|---|---|---|---|---|---|---|---|---|
| soccer | ⚽ | ⚽ | ⚽ | ⚽ | ⚽ | ⚽ | ⚽ | ⚽ | ⚽ | |
| football | 🏈 | 🏈 | 🏈 | 🏈 | 🏈 | | | | | |
| basketball | 🏀 | 🏀 | 🏀 | 🏀 | 🏀 | 🏀 | 🏀 | | | |
| baseball | ⚾ | ⚾ | ⚾ | ⚾ | ⚾ | | | | | |
| | 1 | 2 | 3 | 4 | 5 | 6 | 7 | 8 | 9 | 10 |

1. How many students like soccer? _____

2. How many students like football? _____

3. How many students like basketball? _____

4. How many students like baseball? _____

5. Which sport was the favorite? _____

6. Which two sports were liked by the same number of students?

   _____  _____

**Use the bar graph above to answer questions 7–10.**

7. How many people liked soccer and football?

   _____ + _____ = _____

8. How many students liked basketball and baseball?

   _____ + _____ = _____

9. How many more students liked basketball than baseball?

   _____ – _____ = _____

10. How many more students liked soccer than baseball?

    _____ – _____ = _____

| Started: | Finished: | Total Time: | Completed: | Correct: |
|---|---|---|---|---|

Name _____    Date _____

| Tally Marks | 1 = | | 5 =  | 10 = |
|---|---|---|---|

**Write tally marks for each of the numbers.**

**1.** ( 3 )

**2.** ( 6 )

**3.** ( 9 )

**4.** ( 12 )

**Use tally marks to show the number of objects in each group.**

**5.**

**6.** 

**7.**

**Write the number for each group of tally marks.**

**8.** | | = _____        **9.**  = _____        **10.** 洲| | | = _____

| Started: | Finished: | Total Time: | Completed: | Correct: |
|---|---|---|---|---|

# Interpret Data

Name _____  Date _____

Callie picked flowers last week.  Use the chart to answer questions 1–10.

| Callie's Flowers | |
|---|---|
| **Monday** | 🌼 🌼 🌼 |
| **Tuesday** | 🌼 🌼 🌼 🌼 🌼 |
| **Wednesday** | 🌼 🌼 🌼 🌼 🌼 🌼 🌼 🌼 |
| **Thursday** | 🌼 🌼 🌼 🌼 🌼 🌼 |
| **Friday** | 🌼 🌼 🌼 🌼 🌼 🌼 🌼 🌼 🌼 |

1. How many flowers did Callie pick on Monday? _____

2. How many flowers did she pick on Tuesday? _____

3. How many flowers did she pick on Wednesday? _____

4. How many flowers did she pick on Thursday? _____

5. How many flowers did she pick on Friday? _____

**Choose the correct answer for each question.**

6. Did she pick more than five flowers on Tuesday?    **Yes**        **No**

7. Did she pick more than three flowers on Friday?    **Yes**        **No**

8. Which day did she pick six flowers? _____

9. Which day did she pick the *least* number of flowers?

   **Monday**        **Tuesday**        **Wednesday**        **Thursday**        **Friday**

10. Which day did she pick the *most* flowers?

   **Monday**        **Tuesday**        **Wednesday**        **Thursday**        **Friday**

| Started: | Finished: | Total Time: | Completed: | Correct: |
|---|---|---|---|---|

Name _____        Date _____

**Mrs. Gaylord's class wanted to vote on the next field trip. Use the pictograph below to answer questions 1–10.**

1. How many votes did the aquarium get? _____

2. How many votes did the farm get? _____

3. How many votes did the zoo get? _____

4. How many more votes did the zoo get than the farm?

   _____

5. How many more votes did the aquarium get than the farm?

   _____

**Circle the correct answer.**

6. Which choice got the *most* votes?

   **Aquarium**        **Farm**        **Zoo**

7. Which choice got the *fewest* votes?

   **Aquarium**        **Farm**        **Zoo**

8. Which choice got 5 votes?

   **Aquarium**        **Farm**        **Zoo**

9. Which choice got 7 votes?

   **Aquarium**        **Farm**        **Zoo**

10. Which place would you like to visit?

   **Aquarium**        **Farm**        **Zoo**

| Field Trip Votes | | |
|---|---|---|
| **Aquarium** | **Farm** | **Zoo** |

| Started: | Finished: | Total Time: | Completed: | Correct: |
|---|---|---|---|---|

Name _____     Date _____

**Use the word box to name each plane shape.**

1.    _____

2.    _____

3.    _____

4.    _____

5.    _____

6.    _____

**circle**

**oval**

**rectangle**

**rhombus**

**square**

**triangle**

**How many sides does each shape have?  Circle your answers.**

7. square         0        1        2        3        4

8. triangle       0        1        2        3        4

9. rectangle      0        1        2        3        4

10. circle        0        1        2        3        4

| Started: | Finished: | Total Time: | Completed: | Correct: |
|----------|-----------|-------------|------------|----------|

Name _____ Date _____

## Circle your answers for questions 1–3.

| | | |
|---|---|---|
| **1.** | Which shape is not a circle? |  |
| **2.** | Which shape is not a triangle? |  |
| **3.** | Which shape is not a square? |  |

## Draw the shapes.

| **4.** | **5.** | **6.** |
|---|---|---|
| **square** | **rectangle** | **rhombus** |

## Decide if each shape is *closed* or *open*. Circle your answers.

**7.**     **Closed**        **Open**

**8.**     **Closed**        **Open**

**9.**     **Closed**        **Open**

**10.**     **Closed**        **Open**

| Started: | Finished: | Total Time: | Completed: | Correct: |
|---|---|---|---|---|

Name _____     Date _____

## Cross out the numbers in the circles.  Add the numbers in the squares.

**1.**  (2)  [4]  [6]  (8)

_____ + _____ = _____

**2.**  [3]  (5)  [7]  (9)

_____ + _____ = _____

**3.**  [4]  [7]  (8)  (2)

_____ + _____ = _____

**4.**  (5)  [6]  [5]  (7)

_____ + _____ = _____

**5.**  (8)  [6]  (3)  [6]

_____ + _____ = _____

**6.**  (6)  [3]  (4)  [9]

_____ + _____ = _____

## Use the word bank to help you answer the questions.

> square     triangle     rhombus     rectangle

**7.** Name a shape that has three sides. _____

**8.** Name a shape that has four equal sides. _____

**9.** What is another name for a diamond shape? _____

**10.** Name a shape that has two long sides and two short sides?

_____

| Started: | Finished: | Total Time: | Completed: | Correct: |
|---|---|---|---|---|

# Test 84                                    Geometry

Name _____    Date _____

## Draw a line from each solid shape to its name.

1.                                      **sphere**

2.                                      **rectangular prism**

3.  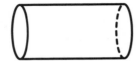                                    **cylinder**

4.  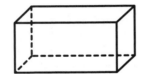                                    **cube**

5.                                      **cone**

## Answer *True* or *False*.

**6.** A cylinder has a circle on each end.          **True**          **False**

**7.** The faces of a cube are all squares.          **True**          **False**

**8.** A cylinder has a point on top.                **True**          **False**

**9.** A sphere has no corners.                      **True**          **False**

**10.** A cone has a point on top.                   **True**          **False**

| Started: | Finished: | Total Time: | Completed: | Correct: |
|----------|-----------|-------------|------------|----------|

Name _____　Date _____

## Use the word box to name each solid shape.

1. 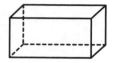 _____

2.  _____

3.  _____

4.  _____

5. _____

| |
|---|
| cone |
| cube |
| cylinder |
| rectangular prism |
| sphere |

## Match the object to each solid shape name.

6. _____

7. _____

8. _____

9. _____

10.  _____

| |
|---|
| cube |
| cylinder |
| rectangular prism |
| sphere |
| cone |

| Started: | Finished: | Total Time: | Completed: | Correct: |
|---|---|---|---|---|

# Test 86 Geometry

Name _____  Date _____

**Circle the shape in each row that is *not* a solid shape.**

1.

2.

3.

**Circle the items in each row that match each solid shape.**

4. cube

5. rectangular prism

6. sphere

7. cylinder

8. cone

**Circle Yes or No.**

| 9. | This is a sphere. | 10. | This is a cube. |
|---|---|---|---|
| Yes  No | | Yes  No | |

Started: Finished: Total Time: Completed: Correct:

*TCR 8079 Timed Math Practice* 90 ©*Teacher Created Resources*

Name _____     Date _____

## Circle the correct answer for each question.  Choose *A* or *B*.

**1.** What does the word symmetry mean?

    **A.** The line divides the picture in the middle.

    **B.** Both sides of the picture are exactly the same.

**2.** Which circle is divided symmetrically?

    **A.**     **B.**

**3.** Which square is divided symmetrically?

    **A.**     **B.**

**4.** Which triangle is divided symmetrically?

    **A.**     **B.**

## Look at the dashed line on each object.  Are the two sides symmetrical?  Circle *Yes* or *No*.

**5.**   **Yes**    **No**

**6.**   **Yes**    **No**

**7.** 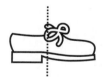  **Yes**    **No**

**8.**   **Yes**    **No**

## Divide each shape symmetrically.

| 9. 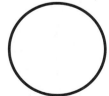 | 10.  |
| --- | --- |

| Started: | Finished: | Total Time: | Completed: | Correct: |
| --- | --- | --- | --- | --- |

# Symmetry

Name _____  Date _____

**Look at the dashed line on each object. Are the two sides symmetrical? Circle *Yes* or *No*.**

1.   Yes    No

2.   Yes    No

3.   Yes    No

4.   Yes    No

**Show two different ways to divide the flower symmetrically.**

5.

6.

**Divide each triangle symmetrically.**

7.

8.

**Divide each rectangle symmetrically.**

9.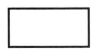

10.

| Started: | Finished: | Total Time: | Completed: | Correct: |
|---|---|---|---|---|

Name _____      Date _____

**Circle the letter next to the shape that is divided symmetrically in each row.**

1.   A.        B.

2.   A.        B.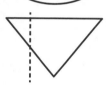

3.   A. 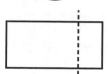       B.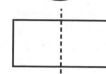

4.   A.        B.

**Look at the dashed line on each object. Are the two sides symmetrical?**
**Circle *Yes* or *No*.**

5.     **Yes**    **No**       6.     **Yes**    **No**

7.     **Yes**    **No**       8. 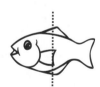    **Yes**    **No**

**Divide each oval symmetrically.**

9. 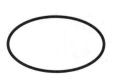          10.

| Started: | Finished: | Total Time: | Completed: | Correct: |
|---|---|---|---|---|

Fractions

Name _____ Date _____

**A fraction is an equal part of a whole.**

Whole          Half

**Circle the letter next to the shape in each row that is divided in half.**

1.   A. 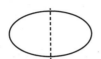          B.

2.   A.           B.

3.   A.           B.

4.   A.           B.

**Draw dots on the other side of each domino to make each half the same.**

5. 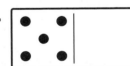          6.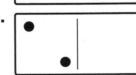

7. 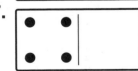          8.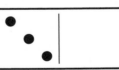

**Circle half of the items in each row.**

9.

10.

| Started: | Finished: | Total Time: | Completed: | Correct: |
|----------|-----------|-------------|------------|----------|

Name _____ Date _____

## Circle the correct fraction for each shaded area.

1.           1/3          2/3          3/3

2.           1/3          2/3          3/3

3.           1/3          2/3          3/3

## Fill in one-third of each shape.

4.           5.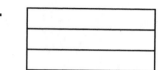

## Match each pie to the correct fraction.  Count the slices that are still left.

6.           1/3          2/3          3/3

7.           1/3          2/3          3/3

8.           1/3          2/3          3/3

## Cross out one-third of the items in each row.

9.

10.

| Started: | Finished: | Total Time: | Completed: | Correct: |
| --- | --- | --- | --- | --- |

Name _____     Date _____

## Circle the correct fraction for each shaded area.

1.      $\dfrac{1}{4}$     $\dfrac{2}{4}$     $\dfrac{3}{4}$     $\dfrac{4}{4}$

2.      $\dfrac{1}{4}$     $\dfrac{2}{4}$     $\dfrac{3}{4}$     $\dfrac{4}{4}$

3.      $\dfrac{1}{4}$     $\dfrac{2}{4}$     $\dfrac{3}{4}$     $\dfrac{4}{4}$

4.      $\dfrac{1}{4}$     $\dfrac{2}{4}$     $\dfrac{3}{4}$     $\dfrac{4}{4}$

## Follow the directions to finish the pizza.

**5.** Divide the pizza in half.

**6.** Divide the pizza again to make 4 quarters.

**7.** Add triangles to half the pizza.

**8.** Add circles to three-quarters of the pizza.

## Cross out one quarter of the items in each row.

9.

10.

| Started: | Finished: | Total Time: | Completed: | Correct: |
|---|---|---|---|---|

Name _____  Date _____

**Use the word box to write the words for each fraction.**

1. $\frac{1}{4}$ _____

2. $\frac{2}{3}$ _____

3. $\frac{1}{3}$ _____

4. $\frac{3}{4}$ _____

5. $\frac{1}{2}$ _____

one-half

one-third

two-thirds

one-fourth

three-fourths

**Follow the directions to find the answers.**

6. Circle the square that shows half of the whole.

   **A.**     **B.**     **C.**

7. Circle the rectangle that shows two-thirds of the whole.

   **A.** 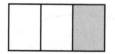    **B.** 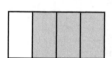    **C.**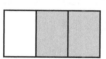

8. Circle the square that shows three-quarters of the whole.

   **A.**     **B.**     **C.**

**Complete the fraction for the shaded part of each set.**

9.  $= \dfrac{\phantom{0}}{4}$

10.  $= \dfrac{\phantom{0}}{3}$

Name _____     Date _____

**Complete the fraction for the shaded part of each set.**

1.

$\frac{\phantom{0}}{4}$

2.

$\frac{\phantom{0}}{4}$

3.

$\frac{\phantom{0}}{3}$

4.

$\frac{\phantom{0}}{3}$

5.

$\frac{\phantom{0}}{4}$

**Fill in half of each shape.**

6.       7.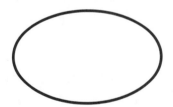

**How much of each shape is shaded? Circle your answers.**

8.     $\frac{1}{3}$     $\frac{2}{3}$     $\frac{3}{3}$

9.     $\frac{1}{4}$     $\frac{1}{2}$     $\frac{1}{3}$

10. 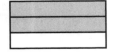    $\frac{1}{3}$     $\frac{2}{3}$     $\frac{3}{3}$

| Started: | Finished: | Total Time: | Completed: | Correct: |
|----------|-----------|-------------|------------|----------|

# Fractions

Name _____  Date _____

## Circle the correct fraction for the shaded part of each square.

1.      $\frac{1}{2}$     $\frac{1}{3}$     $\frac{1}{4}$

2.      $\frac{2}{4}$     $\frac{2}{3}$     $\frac{1}{3}$

3.      $\frac{1}{4}$     $\frac{2}{4}$     $\frac{3}{4}$

4.      $\frac{1}{4}$     $\frac{1}{2}$     $\frac{1}{3}$

## Circle half of the happy faces.

5.

6.

7.

## Circle the correct fraction for the shaded group(s).

8.        $\frac{1}{3}$     $\frac{2}{3}$     $\frac{3}{3}$

9.        $\frac{1}{4}$     $\frac{2}{4}$     $\frac{3}{4}$

10.         $\frac{1}{3}$     $\frac{2}{3}$     $\frac{3}{3}$

| Started: | Finished: | Total Time: | Completed: | Correct: |  |
|---|---|---|---|---|---|

Name _____     Date _____

## How much is each coin worth?  Circle your answers.

1.      1¢          5¢          10¢          25¢

2.      1¢          5¢          10¢          25¢

3.      1¢          5¢          10¢          25¢

4.      1¢          5¢          10¢          25¢

## How much money is in each group?

5.  = _____ ¢

6.  = _____ ¢

7.  = _____ ¢

## Answer the questions.

8. How many pennies equal one nickel? _____

9. How many pennies equal one dime? _____

10. How many pennies equal one quarter? _____

| Started: | Finished: | Total Time: | Completed: | Correct: |
|---|---|---|---|---|

Name _____ Date _____

## Circle the name of each coin.

**1.**     penny      nickel      dime      quarter

**2.**     penny      nickel      dime      quarter

**3.**     penny      nickel      dime      quarter

**4.**     penny      nickel      dime      quarter

## How much money is in each group?

**5.**  +  +  = _____ ¢

**6.**  +  +  = _____ ¢

**7.**  +  +  +  +  = _____ ¢

## Answer *True* or *False*.

**8.**  +  =         **True**      **False**

**9.**  +  +  =         **True**      **False**

**10.**  +  +  +  =         **True**      **False**

| Started: | Finished: | Total Time: | Completed: | Correct: |
|---|---|---|---|---|

Name _____                    Date _____

**Circle the quarters needed for each amount.**

1. 25¢

2. 75¢

3. 50¢

4. $1.00

**Answer *True* or *False*.**

5.                            True     False

6.                           True     False

7.         True     False

8.                            True     False

**Answer the questions.**

9. How many pennies equal a quarter? _____

10. How many nickels equal a quarter? _____

| Started: | Finished: | Total Time: | Completed: | Correct: |
|----------|-----------|-------------|------------|----------|

Name _____ Date _____

## Circle the dimes needed for each amount.

1. 50¢

2. 30¢

3. 70¢

4. 40¢

5. 60¢

## Match the money in each group to the correct total in the box.

6. ⊙ + ⊙ = _____

7. ⊙ + ⊙ + ⊙ = _____

8. ⊙ + ⊙ + ⊙ + ⊙ + ⊙ = _____

9. ⊙ + ⊙ + ⊙ + ⊙ + ⊙ + ⊙ = _____

10. ⊙ + ⊙ + ⊙ + ⊙ + ⊙ + ⊙ + ⊙ = _____

| 10¢ |
| 20¢ |
| 25¢ |
| 15¢ |
| 5¢ |

Started:    Finished:    Total Time:    Completed:    Correct:

Name _____    Date _____

## Circle the nickels needed for each amount.

1. 10¢  

2. 25¢  

3. 15¢  

4. 20¢  

## Use the correct sign (>, <, =) between the two groups of coins in each row.

5.  +  +    ( )    +

6.  +  +    ( )    +

7.  +  +    ( )    +

8.  +  +    ( )    +

## Fill in the blanks to answer the questions.

9. _____ nickels are the same amount of money as 1 dime.

10. _____ nickels are the same amount of money as 1 quarter.

| Started: | Finished: | Total Time: | Completed: | Correct: |
|---|---|---|---|---|

# Common Core State Standards Correlation

Pages in *Timed Math Practice* meet one or more of the following Common Core State Standards © Copyright 2010. National Governors Association Center for Best Practices and Council of Chief State School Officers. All rights reserved. For more information about the Common Core State Standards, go to *http://www.corestandards.org/* or *http://www.teachercreated.com/standards/*.

| Mathematics Standards | Test |
|---|---|
| **Operations & Algebraic Thinking** | |
| **1.OA.1.** Use addition and subtraction within 20 to solve word problems involving situations of adding to, taking from, putting together, taking apart, and comparing, with unknowns in all positions, e.g., by using objects, drawings, and equations with a symbol for the unknown number to represent the problem. | 31–33, 35–36, 40–44, 46, 48, 52–55, 57–60, 64 |
| **1.OA.2.** Solve word problems that call for addition of three whole numbers whose sum is less than or equal to 20, e.g., by using objects, drawings, and equations with a symbol for the unknown number to represent the problem. | 36, 42 |
| **1.OA.3.** Apply properties of operations as strategies to add and subtract. | 34, 48–53, 55–56 |
| **1.OA.4.** Understand subtraction as an unknown-addend problem. *For example, subtract 10 – 8 by finding the number that makes 10 when added to 8.* | 57 |
| **1.OA.5.** Relate counting to addition and subtraction (e.g., by counting on 2 to add 2). | 13, 36, 41–42 |
| **1.OA.6.** Add and subtract within 20, demonstrating fluency for addition and subtraction within 10. Use strategies such as counting on; making ten (e.g., 8 + 6 = 8 + 2 + 4 = 10 + 4 = 14); decomposing a number leading to a ten (e.g., 13 − 4 = 13 − 3 − 1 = 10 − 1 = 9); using the relationship between addition and subtraction (e.g., knowing that 8 + 4 = 12, one knows 12 − 8 = 4); and creating equivalent but easier or known sums (e.g., adding 6 + 7 by creating the known equivalent 6 + 6 + 1 = 12 + 1 = 13). | 2, 4–9, 11–13, 15, 28, 31–60, 64, 96–99 |
| **1.OA.7.** Understand the meaning of the equal sign, and determine if equations involving addition and subtraction are true or false. For example, which of the following equations are true and which are false? 6 = 6, 7 = 8 − 1, 5 + 2 = 2 + 5, 4 + 1 = 5 + 2. | 34–35, 45, 48, 51, 54, 58–60, 97–98 |
| **1.OA.8.** Determine the unknown whole number in an addition or subtraction equation relating three whole numbers. | 2, 4–9, 11–13, 15, 28, 31–60, 64, 96–99 |
| **Number & Operations in Base Ten** | |
| **1.NBT.1.** Count to 120, starting at any number less than 120. In this range, read and write numerals and represent a number of objects with a written numeral. | 4–5, 9, 17, 19, 33, 39, 43, 47, 49–50 |
| **1.NBT.2.** Understand that the two digits of a two-digit number represent amounts of tens and ones and understand special cases. | 10, 12–18, 20–22 |
| **1.NBT.3.** Compare two two-digit numbers based on meanings of the tens and ones digits, recording the results of comparisons with the symbols >, =, and <. | 25–27 |
| **1.NBT.4.** Add within 100, including adding a two-digit number and a one-digit number, and adding a two-digit number and a multiple of 10, using concrete models or drawings and strategies based on place value, properties of operations, and/or the relationship between addition and subtraction; relate the strategy to a written method and explain the reasoning used. Understand that in adding two-digit numbers, one adds tens and tens, ones and ones; and sometimes it is necessary to compose a ten. | 37–39, 41–42, 46, 49, 53, 58–60 |
| **Measurement & Data** | |
| **1.MD.1.** Order three objects by length; compare the lengths of two objects indirectly by using a third object. | 61–63, 68–69 |
| **1.MD.2.** Express the length of an object as a whole number of length units, by laying multiple copies of a shorter object (the length unit) end to end; understand that the length measurement of an object is the number of same-size length units that span it with no gaps or overlaps. | 61–64, 68–69 |
| **1.MD.3.** Tell and write time in hours and half-hours using analog and digital clocks. | 70–75 |
| **1.MD.4.** Organize, represent, and interpret data with up to three categories; ask and answer questions about the total number of data points, how many in each category, and how many more or less are in one category than in another. | 76–80 |
| **Geometry** | |
| **1.G.1.** Distinguish between defining attributes (e.g., triangles are closed and three-sided) versus non-defining attributes (e.g., color, orientation, overall size); build and draw shapes to possess defining attributes. | 82, 85–86 |
| **1.G.3.** Partition circles and rectangles into two and four equal shares, describe the shares using the words *halves*, *fourths*, and *quarters*, and use the phrases *half of*, *fourth of*, and *quarter of*. Describe the whole as two of, or four of the shares. Understand for these examples that decomposing into more equal shares creates smaller shares. | 87–95 |

# Answer Key

**Test 1—Page 5**
1. two
2. five
3. one
4. four
5. three

6. 10; ten
7. 8; eight
8. 9; nine
9. 6; six
10. 7; seven

**Test 2—Page 6**
1. 4
2. 3
3. 5
4. 4
5. 5

6. 3
7. 6
8. 8
9. 10
10. 14

**Test 3—Page 7**
1. 3
2. 1
3. 4
4. 2
5. 5, 1, 9, 11

6. 1, 7, 13, 5
7. 2nd insect
8. 4th insect
9. 1st insect
10. 3rd insect

**Test 4—Page 8**
1. 2
2. 1
3. 3
4. 6
5. 8

6. 5
7. 9
8. 8
9. 12
10. 16

**Test 5—Page 9**
1. second
2. fourth
3. first
4. fifth
5. third
6. 5

7. 7
8. 6
9. **1**, 2, **3**, 4, **5**, 6, **7**, 8, **9**, 10
10. 1, **2**, 3, **4**, 5, **6**, 7, **8**, 9, **10**

**Test 6—Page 10**
1. 4
2. 3
3. 5
4. 5
5. 5

6. 5
7. 10
8. 4
9. 3
10. 5

**Test 7—Page 11**
1. 2
2. 1
3. 3
4. 3
5. 2

6. 1
7. 7
8. 6
9. 9 (circled)
10. 10

**Test 8—Page 12**
1. 4
2. 8
3. 8
4. 10
5. 3

6. 9
7. 9
8. 9
9. 16
10. 18

**Test 9—Page 13**
1. 5
2. 2
3. Check drawing for 10 triangles.
4. 10, **20**, 30, 40, **50**, 60, **70**, 80, **90**, 100
5. 10, 20, **30**, 40, 50, **60**, **70**, 80, **90**, 100
6. 10
7. 10
8. 7 + 3 = 10
9. 5 + 5 = 10
10. 4 + 6 = 10

**Test 10—Page 14**
1. 10
2. 6
3. 3 Tens 5 Ones
4. 7 Tens 3 Ones

5–6.

7. 3 5 7 9
8. 2 4 6 8 10
9. 20
10. 2

**Test 11—Page 15**
1. 10
2. 8
3. 6
4. 7
5. 10

6. 4
7. 9
8. 3
9. 6
10. 2

**Test 12—Page 16**
1. 5
2. 4
3. 8
4. 6
5. 2

6. Circle 3
7. Circle 7
8. Circle 4
9. Circle 9
10. 9

**Test 13—Page 17**
1. 2
2. 6
3. 5
4. 8
5. Circle 4; 40

6. Circle 3; 30
7. 20
8. 40
9. 30
10. 50

**Test 14—Page 18**
1. 5
2. 7
3. 3
4. 60
5. 70

6. 90
7. 40
8. Circle 70
9. Circle 90
10. Circle 80

**Test 15—Page 19**
1. 10 + 3
2. 60 + 8
3. 40 + 5
4. 70 + 9
5. 20 + 1

6. 30 + 6
7. 4 Tens + 9 Ones
8. 8 Tens + 7 Ones
9. 5 Tens + 7 Ones
10. 6 Tens + 3 Ones

# Answer Key (cont.)

## Test 16—Page 20
1. 3 Tens + 5 Ones
2. 8 Tens + 9 Ones
3. 4 Tens + 2 Ones
4. 1 Ten + 1 One
5. 5 Tens + 7 Ones
6. 3 Tens + 8 Ones
7. 1 Ten + 9 Ones
8. 11; 10 + 1
9. 12; 10 + 2
10. 14; 10 + 4

## Test 17—Page 21
1. 10, **20**, 30, **40**, 50, **60**, 70, **80**, 90, 100
2. **10**, 20, **30**, **40**, 50, 60, 70, **80**, 90, 100
3. 10, 20, **30**, 40, **50**, 60, **70**, 80, **90**, 100
4. 10, **20**, 30, 40, 50, **60**, **70**, 80, 90, **100**
5. 20 + 6
6. 30 + 7
7. 40 + 8
8. Circle 30, 50, 20
9. Circle 15, 12, 14
10. Circle 74, 34

## Test 18—Page 22
1. Circle 15, 45, 25
2. Circle 13, 73, 83
3. Circle 99
4. Circle 80
5. Circle 53
6. Circle 27
7. 15; 10 + 5
8. 51; 50 + 1
9. 64; 60 + 4
10. 78; 70 + 8

## Test 19—Page 23
All 10s should be circled.
1. 1, **2**, 3, 4, **5**, 6, 7, 8, 9, **10**
2. 11, 12, **13**, 14, 15, **16**, 17, 18, **19**, 20
3. 21, **22**, 23, **24**, 25, 26, 27, **28**, 29, 30
4. 31, 32, **33**, 34, **35**, 36, **37**, 38, 39, 40
5. **41**, 42, **43**, 44, 45, **46**, 47, 48, 49, 50
6. 51, 52, 53, 54, **55**, 56, **57**, 58, 59, **60**
7. 61, 62, 63, **64**, 65, 66, 67, **68**, **69**, 70
8. 71, 72, **73**, 74, **75**, 76, 77, 78, **79**, 80
9. 81, **82**, 83, 84, 85, **86**, 87, 88, 89, 90
10. **91**, 92, 93, **94**, 95, 96, 97, 98, 99, **100**

## Test 20—Page 24
1. 1
2. 10
3. 50
4. 100
5. 2 hundreds, 3 tens, 9 ones
6. 1 hundred, 7 tens, 5 ones
7. 3 hundreds, 4 tens, 3 ones
8. 9
9. 7
10. 5

## Test 21—Page 25
1. 601
2. 231
3. 508
4. 969
5. 552
6. 255
7. 364
8. 349
9. 156
10. 202

## Test 22—Page 26
1. 653
2. 327
3. 853
4. 194
5. 141
6. 132
7. 550
8. 6
9. 3
10. 10

## Test 23—Page 27
1. 5
2. 7
3. 9
4. 3
5. 20
6. 39
7. 77
8. 99
9. 19, 15, 14, 12, 9
10. 19

## Test 24—Page 28
1. 3
2. 14
3. 10
4. 18
5. 9
6. 30
7. 22
8. 12
9. 8, 11, 16, 18, 20
10. 8

## Test 25—Page 29
1. >
2. <
3. <
4. <
5. >
6. <
7. >
8. 49 > 36
9. 32 > 23
10. 12 < 21

## Test 26—Page 30
1. <
2. >
3. =
4. >
5. <
6. >
7. =
8. <
9. Check answer.
10. Check answer.

## Test 27—Page 31
1. greater than
2. equal to
3. less than
4. 24
5. 28
6. 29
7. 44
8. possible answers:  13 > 3; 30 >13; 30 > 3
9. possible answers:  3 < 13; 13 < 30; 3 < 30
10. possible answers:  3 = 3; 13 = 13; 30 = 30

## Test 28—Page 32
1. Check that 1, 3, 5, 7, and 9 are circled.
2. Check that 2, 4, 6, 8, and 10 are underlined.
3. 10
4. 3
5. 8
6. 7
7. 4
8. 2
9. 19
10. 11

**Test 29—Page 33**
1. Check that 18 and 21 were added to number line.
2. 15
3. 24
4. 22
5. 18
6. Check that 12 and 13 were added to number line.
7. 14
8. 10
9. 18
10. 13

**Test 30—Page 34**
1. 13
2. 14
3. 12
4. 8
5. 3
6. 6
7. 15
8. 20
9. 10
10. 19

**Test 31—Page 35**
1. 5 + 3 = 8
2. 4 + 6 = 10
3. 3 + 3 + 3 = 9
4. 6 + 6 = 12
5. 7
6. 9
7. 10
8. 11
9. 4 + 5 = 9
10. 6 + 3 = 9

**Test 32—Page 36**
1. 5
2. 4
3. 5
4. 5
5. 4 + 3 = 7
6. 4 + 1 = 5
7. 2 + 2 = 4
8. 2 + 3 = 5
9. 2 + 2 = 4
10. 2 + 1 = 3

**Test 33—Page 37**
1. 5 + 2 = 7
2. 6 + 4 = 10
3. 4 + 2 = 6
4. 3 + 6 = 9
5. 7
6. 9
7. 8
8. 10
9. 5 + 3 = 8
10. 4 + 6 = 10

**Test 34—Page 38**
1. 10
2. 10
3. 7; 3
4. 10; 7
5. 9; 4
6. 8; 6
7. True
8. False
9. True
10. 10– Check the circle sets.

**Test 35—Page 39**
1. False
2. True
3. True
4. 10
5. 8
6. 4
7. 6
8. 4 + 6 = 10
9. 4 + 5 = 9
10. 5 + 5 = 10

**Test 36—Page 40**
1. 5
2. 6
3. 7
4. 8
5. 9
6. 8
7. 9
8. 9
9. 2 + 2 + 2 + 2 = 8
10. 2 + 2 + 2 + 2 + 2 + 2 = 12

**Test 37—Page 41**
1. 13
2. 15
3. 12
4. 14
5. 15
6. 13
7. 14
8. 6
9. 10
10. 7

**Test 38—Page 42**
1. 16
2. 19
3. 17
4. 18
5. 19
6. 16
7. 17
8. 4
9. 5
10. 8

**Test 39—Page 43**
1. 2, **4**, 6, **8**, 10, **12**, 14, **16**, **18**, 20
2. 5, **10**, 15, **20**, 25, **30**, 35, **40**, 45, **50**
3. 3, **6**, 9, **12**, 15, **18**, 21, **24**, 27, **30**
4. 16 (Circle 5 and 5.)
5. 17 (Circle 8 and 2.)
6. 19 (Circle 6 and 4.)
7. 13 (Circle 7 and 3.)
8. 16
9. 14
10. 18

**Test 40—Page 44**
1. 17
2. 12
3. 14
4. 13
5. 15
6. 14
7. 12
8. 16
9. 6 + 9 = 15
10. 9 + 9 = 18

**Test 41—Page 45**
1. 19
2. 37
3. 18
4. 59
5. 28
6. 18
7. 55
8. 80
9. 22 + 7 = 29
10. 42 + 6 = 48

**Test 42—Page 46**
1. 39
2. 48
3. 97
4. 68
5. 79
6. 84
7. 70
8. 100
9. 20 + 8 = 28
10. 6 + 5 + 2 = 13

## Test 43—Page 47

1. $10 - 5 = 5$
2. $8 - 7 = 1$
3. $8 - 3 = 5$
4. $10 - 4 = 6$
5. 3
6. 5
7. 2
8. 6
9. $10 - 3 = 7$
10. $9 - 7 = 2$

## Test 44—Page 48

1. 6
2. 4
3. 4
4. 0
5. 1
6. 3
7. 0
8. 2
9. $9 - 3 = 6$
10. $12 - 7 = 5$

## Test 45—Page 49

1. 2
2. 5
3. 8
4. 4
5. 6
6. 7
7. 6
8. 7
9. True
10. False

## Test 46—Page 50

1. 8
2. 5
3. 4
4. 6
5. 7
6. 5
7. 9
8. 9
9. $12 - 6 = 6$
10. $10 - 3 = 7$

## Test 47—Page 51

1. $15 - 5 = 10$
2. $12 - 3 = 9$
3. $20 - 7 = 13$
4. $20 - 4 = 16$
5. 10
6. 10
7. 9
8. 8
9. 9
10. 9

## Test 48—Page 52

1–2. $9 - 4 = 5$; $9 - 5 = 4$
3–4. $10 - 7 = 3$; $10 - 3 = 7$
5. False
6. True
7. False
8. True
9. $14 - 8 = 6$
10. $15 - 11 = 4$

## Test 49—Page 53

1. $18 - 7 = 11$
2. $18 - 9 = 9$
3. 9
4. 10
5. 9
6. 9
7–8. $10 - 4 = 6$; $10 - 6 = 4$
9–10. $13 - 5 = 8$; $13 - 8 = 5$

## Test 50—Page 54

1. 11
2. 15
3. 15
4. 13
5. $15 - 9 = 6$
6. $13 - 7 = 6$
7–8. $12 - 4 = 8$; $12 - 8 = 4$
9–10. $13 - 9 = 4$; $13 - 4 = 9$

## Test 51—Page 55

1–2. $11 - 4 = 7$; $11 - 7 = 4$
3–4. $15 - 7 = 8$; $15 - 8 = 7$
5. True
6. False
7. True
8. True
9. 6
10. 8

## Test 52—Page 56

1. 12
2. 14
3. 20
4. 18
5–6. $19 - 9 = 10$; $19 - 10 = 9$
7–8. $17 - 9 = 8$; $17 - 8 = 9$
9. $19 - 16 = 3$
10. $16 - 8 = 8$

## Test 53—Page 57

1–2. $18 - 15 = 3$; $18 - 3 = 15$
3–4. $16 - 7 = 9$; $16 - 9 = 7$
5. 11
6. 10
7. 7
8. 8
9. $20 - 10 = 10$
10. $18 - 12 = 6$

## Test 54—Page 58

1. 12
2. 16
3. 14
4. 20
5. True
6. False
7. True
8. True
9. $14 - 7 = 7$
10. $16 - 5 = 11$

## Test 55—Page 59

1. 8
2. 7
3. 4
4. 4
5. 10
6. 10
7. 7
8. 3
9. $3 + 4 = 7$; Addition
10. $5 - 2 = 3$; Subtraction

## Test 56—Page 60

1. 10
2. 9
3. 7
4. 2
5. 10
6. 8
7. 10
8. 2
9. $4 + 2 = 6$ triangles
10. $10 - 6 = 4$ squares

## Test 57—Page 61

1. 15
2. 11
3. 7
4. 9
5. 13
6. 13
7. 6
8. 7
9. $12 - 9 = 3$; Subtraction
10. $8 + 7 = 15$; Addition

**Test 58—Page 62**
1. 15
2. 14
3. 12
4. 8
5. 5
6. 6
7. False
8. True
9. True
10. $12 - 6 = 6$; Subtraction

**Test 59—Page 63**
1. 18
2. 20
3. 19
4. 8
5. 12
6. 6
7. True
8. False
9. $7 + 9 = 16$; Addition
10. $16 - 8 = 8$; Subtraction

**Test 60—Page 64**
1. 9
2. 8
3. 9
4. 7
5. 17
6. 16
7. True
8. True
9. False
10. $16 - 9 = 7$; Subtraction

**Test 61—Page 65**
1. A
2. B
3. B
4. A
5. False
6. True
7. B
8. yards
9. feet
10. inches

**Test 62—Page 66**
1. A
2. B
3. A
4. B
5. Check drawing.
6. Check drawing.
7. house for people
8. horse
9. elephant
10. mouse

**Test 63—Page 67**
1. smaller
2. larger
3. smaller
4. larger
5. ocean
6. hill
7. Check drawing.
8. Check drawing.
9. Check drawing.
10. triangle

**Test 64—Page 68**
1. shorter
2. short
3. shortest
4. tallest
5. taller
6. tall
7. Check answer.
8. Check answer.
9. Check answer.
10. $10 - 7 = 3$

**Test 65—Page 69**
1. fish
2. flower
3. shark
4. cat
5. laundry basket with clothes
6. wheelbarrow with sand
7. slipper
8. balloon
9. empty glass
10. pencil

**Test 66—Page 70**
1. C
2. quart
3. pint
4. gallon
5. B
6. C
7. False
8. True
9. False
10. True

**Test 67—Page 71**
1. A
2. B
3. C
4. B
5. C
6. Check thermometer fill-in.
7. Check thermometer fill-in.
8. Check thermometer fill-in.
9. shorts; tank top
10. hat; scarf

**Test 68—Page 72**
1. 4
2. $4 + 4 = 8$
3. A
4. B
5. Circle last watering can.
6. Cross out middle watering can.
7. Draw box around first watering can.
8. B. football
9. A. pencil
10. B. cat

**Test 69—Page 73**
1. C
2. A
3. D
4. B
5. bike
6. desk
7. watermelon
8. backpack
9. Circle top chain.
10. Cross out middle chain.

**Test 70—Page 74**
1. a day
2. a month
3. a year
4. A
5. B
6. B
7. A
8. B
9. B
10. A

**Test 71—Page 75**
1. A. 12:00
2. B. 2:00
3. A. 9:00
4. B. 7:00
5. B. 5:00
6. B. 11:00
7. True
8. True
9. Check clock hands.
10. Check clock hands.

**Test 72—Page 76**
1. D
2. A
3. B
4. I
5. G
6. C
7. J
8. H
9. E
10. F

**Test 73—Page 77**
1. 7:00
2. 3:00
3. 9:00
4. 8:00
5. 1:00
6. 4:00
7. 12:00
8. 2:00
9. 5:00
10. 10:00

**Test 74—Page 78**
1. I
2. F
3. B
4. C
5. G
6. J
7. A
8. H
9. E
10. D

**Test 75—Page 79**
1–8. Check hands on clocks.
9. A
10. B

**Test 76—Page 80**
1. 8
2. 卌 |||
3. 10
4. 卌 卌
5. slip-ons
6. tie shoes
7. 4
8. 9
9. 7
10. 6

**Test 77—Page 81**
1. 9
2. 5
3. 7
4. 5
5. soccer
6. football and baseball
7. 9 + 5 = 14
8. 7 + 5 = 12
9. 7 – 5 = 2
10. 9 – 5 = 4

**Test 78—Page 82**
1. |||
2. 卌 |
3. 卌 ||||
4. 卌 卌 ||
5. ||||
6. 卌 ||
7. 卌 卌
8. 2
9. 5
10. 8

**Test 79—Page 83**
1. 3
2. 5
3. 8
4. 6
5. 9
6. No
7. Yes
8. Thursday
9. Monday
10. Friday

**Test 80—Page 84**
1. 9
2. 5
3. 7
4. 7 – 5 = 2
5. 9 – 5 = 4
6. Aquarium
7. Farm
8. Farm
9. Zoo
10. Answers will vary.

**Test 81—Page 85**
1. circle
2. square
3. rhombus
4. triangle
5. oval
6. rectangle
7. 4
8. 3
9. 4
10. 0

**Test 82—Page 86**
1. oval
2. rhombus
3. rectangle
4. Check drawing.
5. Check drawing.
6. Check drawing.
7. Closed
8. Open
9. Closed
10. Open

**Test 83—Page 87**
1. 4 + 6 = 10
2. 3 + 7 = 10
3. 4 + 7 = 11
4. 6 + 5 = 11
5. 6 + 6 = 12
6. 3 + 9 = 12
7. triangle
8. square or rhombus
9. rhombus
10. rectangle

**Test 84—Page 88**
1. cone
2. cube
3. cylinder
4. rectangular prism
5. sphere
6. True
7. True
8. False
9. True
10. True

**Test 85—Page 89**
1. rectangular prism
2. cone
3. cube
4. cylinder
5. sphere
6. sphere
7. cylinder
8. cube
9. rectangular prism
10. cone

**Test 86—Page 90**
1. square
2. rectangle
3. circle
4. block, die, and block
5. shoe box, cereal box, and book
6. baseball, volleyball, and soccer ball
7. vase, soup can, and cookie package
8. safety cone, ice cream cone, and party hat
9. Yes
10. No

**Test 87—Page 91**
1. B
2. A
3. B
4. A
5. No
6. Yes
7. No
8. Yes
9. Check answer.
10. Check answer.

**Test 88—Page 92**
1. Yes
2. No
3. No
4. Yes
5. Check answer.
6. Check answer.
7. Check answer.
8. Check answer.
9. Check answer.
10. Check answer.

**Test 89—Page 93**
1. A
2. B
3. A
4. A
5. Yes
6. No
7. Yes
8. No
9. Check answer.
10. Check answer.

**Test 90—Page 94**
1. A
2. B
3. B
4. A
5. Check answer.
6. Check answer.
7. Check answer.
8. Check answer.
9. Circle 4 cars.
10. Circle 3 skateboards.

**Test 91—Page 95**
1. 2/3
2. 2/3
3. 1/3
4. Check answers.
5. Check answers.
6. 1/3
7. 3/3
8. 2/3
9. Cross out 3 hats.
10. Cross out 2 hats.

**Test 92—Page 96**
1. 1/4
2. 4/4
3. 2/4
4. 3/4
5–8. Check pizza.
9. Cross out 1 banana.
10. Cross out 2 pears.

**Test 93—Page 97**
1. one-fourth
2. two-thirds
3. one-third
4. three-fourths
5. one-half
6. B
7. C
8. C
9. 2/4
10. 2/3

**Test 94—Page 98**
1. 1/4
2. 3/4
3. 1/3
4. 1/3
5. 2/4
6. Check shading.
7. Check shading.
8. 1/3
9. 1/2
10. 2/3

**Test 95—Page 99**
1. 1/2
2. 2/3
3. 2/4
4. 1/3
5. Circle 2 faces.
6. Circle 4 faces.
7. Circle 3 faces.
8. 2/3
9. 1/4
10. 1/3

**Test 96—Page 100**
1. 1¢
2. 5¢
3. 10¢
4. 25¢
5. 3¢
6. 20¢
7. 50¢
8. 5
9. 10
10. 25

**Test 97—Page 101**
1. nickel
2. penny
3. quarter
4. dime
5. 20
6. 36
7. 14
8. True
9. True
10. False

**Test 98—Page 102**
1. Circle 1 quarter.
2. Circle 3 quarters.
3. Circle 2 quarters.
4. Circle 4 quarters.
5. True
6. False
7. True
8. False
9. 25
10. 5

**Test 99—Page 103**
1. Circle 5 dimes.
2. Circle 3 dimes.
3. Circle 7 dimes.
4. Circle 4 dimes.
5. Circle 6 dimes.
6. 20¢
7. 15¢
8. 5¢
9. 10¢
10. 25¢

**Test 100—Page 104**
1. Circle 2 nickels.
2. Circle 5 nickels.
3. Circle 3 nickels.
4. Circle 4 nickels.
5. >
6. <
7. =
8. >
9. 2
10. 5